Architects' Guide

Fee bidding still generates emotive reactions from within many sections of the architectural profession. Fee bidding is not taught in most schools of architecture, so practitioners generally rely on hunches and guesswork. It is these wild card guesses that exacerbate the poor levels of income for which the architectural profession is renowned.

This book introduces practising architects, architectural managers and senior students, to the philosophy and practice of analytical estimating for fees. By means of a detailed case study it illustrates the many problems that may be encountered in the calculation of fees for professional services. It gives a step-by-step guide through the complexities of fee bidding and acts as a source of reference to successful bidding. A detailed discussion of the philosophy of design management and architectural management is developed as a backdrop to the preparation of a bid. It leads the reader through the mysteries of converting the calculation of a bid into a serious tender.

This unique text is an essential guide for all practitioners, particularly those at the commencement of their careers and Part 3 students. It will be of importance to all construction professionals who operate within a highly competitive market.

M. Paul Nicholson MSc, PhD, MCIArb has had a wide and varied career in the construction industry, including running his own business, where his experience encompassed all types of buildings. He has been closely involved in the innovative Masters course in Architectural Briefing at the University of Sheffield, the MSc in Construction Procurement at Nottingham Trent University, and the unique MA course in Architectural Management at the University of Nottingham. Dr Nicholson is a Visiting Professor who lectures at universities in many parts of the world, and continues to develop Architectural Management within the architectural and construction professions.

Architects' Guide to Fee Bidding

M. Paul Nicholson

London and New York

First published 2003
by Spon Press
11 New Fetter Lane, London EC4P 4EE

Simultaneously published in the USA and Canada
by Routledge
29 West 35th Street, New York, NY 10001

Spon Press is an imprint of the Taylor & Francis Group

© 2003 M. Paul Nicholson

Typeset in Gill Sans Light by M Rules
Printed and bound in Great Britain by
St Edmundsbury Press, Bury St Edmunds, Suffolk

British Library Cataloguing-in-Publication Data
A catalogue record for this book is available from the British Library

Library of Congress Cataloging-in-Publication Data
Nicholson, M. P. (M. Paul), 1935–
    Architects' guide to fee bidding / M. Paul Nicholson.
        p.   cm.
    Includes bibliographical references and index.
    1. Architects – Fees.   2. Architectural contracts – Estimates.
    3. Letting of contracts.   I. Title.
    NA1996 .N53 2002
    720'.68'1 – dc21   2002070710

ISBN 0–415–27335–8 (hbk)
ISBN 0–415–27336–6 (pbk)

Contents

Preface

It was while undertaking the research for this book that one very senior architect was interviewed. He proudly admitted to being 100 years old and that he had been a practising architect all of his working life. The interview went well until fee bidding was mentioned. This subject was anathema to him, for he strongly believed that all architects should work to the scale of fees and that competition by standards of service and quality of architecture should be the only criteria for proper competition.

In an article in the *Architect's Journal* (*AJ*) on 21 June 2001, Clive Walker suggested that architects could face fines or even gaol for anticompetitive practices. He was referring to the government's statement entitled 'Enterprise for All – The Challenge for the Next Parliament', which proposed that architects should be exempt from competition laws. Under these proposals, the government aims to eliminate price rigging and enhance service quality across all professions.

Previously, Robert Booth in a similar article in the *AJ* (8 March 2001) stated that the 'RIBA claims that the indicative fee scales are not used for anticompetitive price fixing.' Quoting John Vickers, Head of the Office of Fair Trading (OFT), Booth wrote, 'My feeling, very much, is that the principles of competition and application of competition law should be the same across the board.' No doubt, this argument of competition and forms of competition will rage on for a considerable time. The lowest price is rarely the cheapest job, and competition by price alone can only lower the quality of architectural services and fee incomes. If architects can change their image from being service providers to adding value to designs, then salaries within the profession could become more realistic.

This book, being the first within the subject of architects' fee bidding, is, by its nature, experimental. No doubt, architects may differ in their approaches to fee bidding and the use to which they use the calculations. The author will be pleased to receive correspondence that may prove helpful in the production of further editions of this book.

M. Paul Nicholson
Alverton, Nottinghamshire, 2001

Acknowledgements

Much of this book is based on experiential learning, those tenders which were lost or came in a close second in the tender list. There can be no substitute for experience in the preparation of fee bids, but I would be remiss in not paying my respects to those lecturers at the former Brixton School of Architecture and Building. It was those very experienced estimators who painstakingly took students through the minutiae of analytical estimating and who converted me from being a sporting gambler to a serious student of the bidding process.

This book has been written with the help of James Marson BA (Hons), MArch, RIBA. He has painstakingly produced the detailed analysis for our case study and provided the inspiration for this book. My extreme gratitude is offered to him for his exemplary work. Writing this book has been rather like producing a fee bid – there is never enough time to relax and consider the detail. If there are errors in this work, let us hope they are compensating errors, and please accept my apologies.

Technology has transpired against my secretary of many years, Lesley Chester, while typing up my manuscripts. Her machine suffered from a combination of crashes, a virus and failure of the hard drive, yet she still persisted – and won: thank you Lesley. However, her frustration was, in no small part, alleviated by Jayne Riley who picked up the pieces (literally) and restored a level of sanity to the process.

Introduction

> To be an architect takes curiosity and a degree of naivety; I think you have to be an absolutely hopeless optimist, otherwise I don't think you'd ever survive.
> (Lord Foster of Thameside, *Daily Telegraph*, 16 January 1999)

Fee bidding by architects has been variously described as 'wild guesses', 'shots in the dark', 'approximations' or just a 'gamble'. Attempts have been made by the RIBA to give advice to both clients and practitioners of what a sensible bid may consist. Scales of charges have been rigorously applied in the belief that architects would compete only on the quality of their architecture and the professionalism of their organizations. While the entire profession strictly adhered to these scales, all was well and architects flourished.

It was the Monopolies Commission that publicly questioned the practice of the profession-wide standard charges for services, so the mandatory printed scales were withdrawn and replaced with 'recommended' scales as a guide for general use. With one eye on these fee scales, architects were encouraged by their clients to offer fee bids, either as a percentage of the building cost or as a lump sum fixed price. All bids were placed below the 'recommended' fee scales, including some wild-card nil bids.

Not having effective cost records from previous jobs, architectural practices were in many cases forced to enter the world of economic competition without reliable information on which to base a tender. Neither was there any tradition within the profession of calculating fees and managing risk.

This book attempts to encourage practising architects to take their first steps in calculating fee bids. It further proposes the use of this information as a control during the progress of the design. The principles expounded may be adapted to a job in any location. The basic philosophy of risk control is very simple – break down all areas of uncertainty into small elements that can be understood. Clearly, experience of past glories and failures will condition any response, but the novice may gain confidence by analysing each small step in the process. By building up each manageable portion of the design process, the understanding of the whole will become more apparent, and the final figures will be more reliable.

Fee bidding should not be seen in any way as an inhibitor of good design. 'Administration is generally acknowledged as a mundane fact of life, common to both (architectural) manager and professional, but it has remained peripheral to the motivational ambitions of architectural practice' (Allinson 1993). Most schools of architecture in the UK treat matters of finance or financial controls with apparent contempt. Schools, rightly, are concentrating on standards of excellence in design, but without acknowledging the imperative that architecture is a business. No longer can architects rely on royal or aristocratic patronage, as their clients are now the proletariat classes and industrialists. Clients view buildings as commercial necessities that will be demolished when their economic justification is ended.

This work is offered to the architectural profession in the hope that it will provide a lifeline to successful architects and guarantee of continuing design excellence.

Part II introduces the notion of analytical fee calculation. It uses a fairly complex building as an example so that a number of issues can be explored. The building is a university laboratory and teaching building, set somewhere in the South West of England. The model includes both new and alteration building work within a tight and fairly constrained site.

A step-by-step analysis of each move through the estimating process is undertaken, together with a running commentary. Finally, a discussion is promoted about the conversion of a fee bid calculation into a winning bid.

Although inflation, bank interest and rates of exchange are liable to fluctuate, this work has endeavoured to keep pace with the situation in the summer of 2001. All variations from this date should be taken into account.

Part I Commercial professionalism

Design

Management

Design and build

Bids and fees

Competition is good for you

One of the core beliefs of the capitalist system is that competition improves the breed. In 'Yes, we have no competition', Pawley (1998) wrote:

> In the heyday of public-sector architecture after the Second World War, competition was even claimed to justify the mandatory fee scale. The idea was that if all architects charged the same fees for the same work, they would compete on merit alone. Oddly enough, during the Thatcher years, the official view of this cosy arrangement changed. The mandatory fee scale was dismissed as an anti-competitive professional cartel and, as we all know, overt fee competition soon became the bottom line of competition.

Nevertheless, fee scales are still very much in evidence, although they are officially described as indicative fee scales. Their very existence provides a fallback position for novice architects and clients alike, which does nothing to encourage practices to explore the realities of calculated fee bidding.

It was only about five or six years ago that architects felt threatened by the large firms with big resources that could appear to work for minimal fees – thus bringing their apparent fees down to understandable levels. These fears gradually subsided because the architectural profession began to adjust to new conditions of engagement as Pawley (1998) pointed out:

> Rather than suffer the iron rule of the marketplace, they found instead a way of neutralising its effects. Instead of the few architectural competitions and many direct commissions of the post-war years, there were suddenly many architectural competitions and few direct commissions – again, not because competition was succeeding, but because it was failing. Today competition is managed. It is brokered by master-planners, project managers, consultants and contractors so that architects appear to compete when really they are collaborating.

The architectural profession developed gradually from being master-builders and house developers forming, by the nineteenth century, an élitist tightly knit body of design professionals 'to drive out the charlatans from within, and to protect from the charlatans from without'. About a century later, the Monopolies and Mergers Commission tramped through the adjacent professions, which forced the Royal Institute of British Architects (RIBA) to reconsider its position rapidly. In an act of unprecedented bravery, in 1982 the RIBA removed its protectionist policies at one stroke and joined the modern world of industry and competition. Out went advertising restrictions and fee scales, in came unfettered competition, commercial freedom and an opportunity to integrate into the construction industry.

Restrictive professional practices and complacent attitudes came under widespread attack. In 1962, the British Government investigated architects' fees. The Prices and Incomes Board began a twenty-year period of acrimonious discussions that finally resulted in defeat for the profession, which then changed the Code of Engagement and Conduct that, for the first time, severely undermined the monopolistic position attained before the War. Yet, in spite of their monopolistic protection, the Pilkington Report (1956) had identified that architects earned less than most professionals and others in the construction industry.

In a letter to the Editor of the *Architects' Journal*, Tim McArtney (2000) wrote:

Fee levels for the majority of mainstream practices are still too low. The Design and Build industry depresses fees and there is far too much front-end design work being undertaken by the [architectural] profession for little or no reward. This is serious because it leads to a devaluation of the single most important process where the architect adds real value – the ability to solve problems through design flair. Private Finance Initiatives (PFI) have compounded the situation and many practices are having to undertake large amounts of work at risk if they want to be in the significant end of the public sector markets.

He continued:

Fee bidding, for projects being advertised in the *OJEC Journal* is absolutely lethal; we know of some practices bidding as low as 2% for highly complex, lengthy medical building projects requiring a level of professional input which this sort of fee cannot possibly provide. Both parties are irresponsible in this instance – the consultant for whom the bidding is suicidal and the client body for accepting his price knowing, cynically, that the consultant will lose money, or, worse still, fail, but complacently believing that authority has driven down its initial costs and satisfied standing orders. Best Value bidding may go some way to alleviating this state of affairs but I doubt if the conditioned reflexes of some audit-driven hospital trusts and university estates departments will understand the criteria or bother to apply them. The concept of 'partnering' on a long-term basis to improve the quality of the built environment will take many years to break down the arbitrary financial rules that public authorities have erected around themselves.

McArtney then referred to the Ministry of Defence (MOD) and the Public Audit Office as prime movers in the evangelistic movement to re-engineer the construction industry, which would benefit from discontinuous change rather than from an extension of past practices.

A strong response to McArtney's letter was provided by Hugh Wright (2000):

> I read with interest Tim McArtney's letter and make the following observations [. . .] Architects lack clout when negotiating fees. The RIBA's survey of fees as listed in the SFA Guide (1992 edition) has lacked credibility with clients, and is therefore generally disregarded by them. A Housing Association in January 2000 insisted on using the 'Purple Book', RIBA Conditions of Engagement (1979 revision; originally 1971), for appointing consultants of another discipline. The maximum rate stipulated by the same Housing Association for additional work by a principal was £25, excluding VAT per hour. The sum of £500 will not even pay for four hours of a solicitor based in Liverpool on planning matters.

Wright concluded that architects lacked an 'august body' to stand up for them. He complained that the RIBA had its priorities in the wrong arenas; it should be getting the message across on behalf of architects for fees, and making comparisons with other professions such as accountants, doctors, engineers and, especially, lawyers.

Without the protection of a price-fixing monopolistic system, the architectural profession has to bid in an open market. The only protection given by law is (in the UK) the protection of title – 'architect'. The function of designing buildings as a process is open for competition from within and from without the architectural profession. It appears that not only are the clients in a position to dictate terms, but also the profession itself should treat architecture as a profession and as a business, not just as an exciting and liberating vocation.

Architects generally practise in a world where professional boundaries are blurring: in Japan, the Fair Trade Commission challenged an attempt by the architects' association to fix fees for its members; in Germany, the Cartel Office opposed attempts to restrict fee cutting; in Sweden, fees had to become recommended rather than mandatory; in Denmark, fees had to be reduced; in the USA, the American Institute of Architects (AIA) ban on competitive fees was rescinded. Areas of interest are overlapping and the traditional professional markets are merging under pressure from international competition, deregulation and a degree of societal impatience with Victorian notions of professionalism.

In 1985, the Organisation for Economic Co-operation and Development (OECD) referred to middle-class occupations of high status (and high fees) that were market-sheltered by statutory protection. It described the architectural profession as 'the provision of intellectual or specialized skill on a personal, direct basis, based on extensive educational training. In addition, professions are generally subject to controlled and restricted entry, and organization and regulation through professional associations.' In the UK, the statutory body, the Architects' Registration Board (ARB) exists to regulate educational and professional competencies and the title of 'architect'. The RIBA assists the ARB in upholding standards of education and professional ethics as well as acting as an international focus for architectural qualities and a forum for the development of the architectural profession. It has to be viewed from the outside as a learned society whilst supporting its members in their need for a trade union – clearly a dilemma for any organization. Whilst appearing to act in unison, the RIBA and ARB have opposing motives – the ARB exists to protect the British public by the maintenance of high standards of competence, which keeps numbers of practitioners to a minimum, while the RIBA is ever striving to enlarge its critical mass by increasing the volume of members. One is restricting growth by quality constraints, the other needs numbers to survive.

One illustration of client power was described by J. R. LeGood (2000), again in the *Architects' Journal* letters columns, in which the request for design tenders for a house extension (single-storey garage, porch and kitchen – completed 'sometime this year or next'), included the following request for information:

- What services are you able to offer? For example, do you provide a planning service, including design, gaining planning permission and obtaining building regulation approval? Do you also provide 'overseeing' and inspection services during the construction?
- Are you able to provide a free quotation?
- Do you offer a firm price quotation? If not, is the final price likely to vary significantly from the quotation? Do you offer a price limit to a percentage variance?
- Are you able to offer a detailed breakdown of the price quotation?
- What accreditation and/or association membership do you hold?
- How long has your business been established?
- What guarantees and warranties do you offer?
- Are you able to provide references of recently completed work?
- Any other relevant information.

These are genuine and obvious concerns of any client. Possibly in this case the client had suffered previously at the hands of an architect who offered a low quotation, who then found that the only way to show a profit (or even cover costs) was to reduce the levels of service and/or increase the fees. The architect in question would have been well advised politely to decline to tender, or to face these worries squarely and offer a full price that took all the client's questions into account.

In fact, LeGood replied saying that, 'For what is a major investment on your property, I would respectfully suggest that your choice of architect should be driven by quality and value for money, not cost.' (Trust me, I am an architect!) For every vexatious client claiming against a beleaguered architect, there are aggrieved clients suffering from the depredations of unscrupulous architects. It is apparent that there is an unacceptable underbelly of the architectural profession who are not caring, sharing, creative, innovative, sustainable architects, but who steer a tightrope course between maximizing commercial imperatives and narrow interpretations of professional responsibilities to the detriment of their client's immediate interests and the longer term interests of the profession.

There is no evidence to prove Pawley's assertion that 'competition improves the breed'. Indeed, for the majority of architectural practices, the temporary removal of the supporting mandatory fee scale has further depressed the income of an already financially challenged profession.

Design

Design communication

Any author of a piece of directed study, or a student who is entering the field for the first time, will probably expect first to consider the imperative of a definition. What is 'design'? What does 'management' mean? Is there any synergy produced by coupling design with management?

> *Design*: 'A plan or scheme formed in the mind.'
>
> (Chambers and Chambers 1983)

As design is a function of the mind, then it would be right to ask whether design is implicit in all the actions of creative man. Similarly, to what extent is design instinctive or an inherited skill, or gained through exposure and experience? The craft and skill of painting, for example, can be taught. The great masters have all had their apprentices to whom they taught technique, the use of colour and so on. In India, there are several 'artists' villages' which are communes of artists (and their families) who live and work together to develop and share their skills and knowledge.

Examples from nature may indicate that in fact design is instinctive. Consider the intricacy of a bird's nest, or the modular formation of a beehive, or the engineering beauty of a spider's web. All are fashioned instinctively over generations, yet they are not innovative: they only repeat the patterns from the past. Man has the ability to use his instinctive skills and develop them in a creative and progressive way by using his natural talents and an open mind.

However, the proposal that design can be developed or taught implies immediately the imposition of a third party – a tutor who was himself 'directed' in his formative years by others who had their own baggage of tradition and standards from their past.

Lawson (1997) suggested that to 'attempt a definition of design too soon might easily lead to a narrow and restricted view. To understand fully the nature of design, it is necessary not only to seek out the similarities between different design situations, but also to recognise the very real differences'. Any definition of 'design' is likely to be controversial. Chris Jones (1970) gave what he regarded as the 'ultimate definition of design':

'To initiate change in man-made things.'

Such an interpretation denies the richness of design, the delight, the functionality, the originality, the simplicity and the commercial creativity within a 'good design'. Indeed, it ignores the opportunities of a designer to produce an added value to a wealth of natural materials.

> *Management*: 'Art or act of managing, manner of directing or of using anything.'
> (Chambers and Chambers 1983)

It may be reasonable to suggest that the analogy of the birds and the bees can give a clue to the basis of management. First, there is the discipline of self-management – that lonely situation in which a single person, animal or insect undertakes a single activity (the spider's web), the only constraint being that it must be completed to a time due, perhaps to an impending event, for example the arrival of the next generation, or just to survive. However, most activities are undertaken by more than one person; management is frequently a group activity in which roles and communication lines are established and the design parameters set.

Take as an example a pair of swallows that make their nests out of mud and stones. They must mutually agree on the site, their knowledge of construction appears to be instinctive and the nest is built on time. Yet legion are the examples of birds that have started to construct their nests and then stopped, moved a few feet along the roof and then completed their new home. There must have been some communication between the birds to agree to the first site, to start construction and then to abandon the site for one similar in all respects to the former and yet only a short distance away. Therefore, one of the primary essentials of management must be the ability to communicate between the parties; also, that some level of control and understanding exists.

The more complex lives of bees in a hive are completely dependent upon lines of communication for effectiveness and good order. The workers and the drones, together with the queen, all know their stations and roles within their community. Some forage for pollen, some collect nectar, some stand guard on the hive, others feed the young while their relatives construct new combs in which to store the winter food. Besides the routine jobs that must be instinctive, there are day-to-day, minute-by-minute instructions that give definition to the routine activities. Where is the pollen; which direction from the hive; which angle from the sun; how far away? All of these instructions are given by returning bees, using their own unique system of communication, to those departing for fresh supplies.

Therefore, the most elementary situation in which a group activity has to be managed needs an understanding of the language, communication, job, work definitions and roles, and control before, during and on completion of the activity, and an acceptance by the players of the rules of the game. The management of any system of procedure is entirely dependent upon this acceptance of the rules. Everybody in an organization knows who is superior (and therefore has authority); each knows who are the subordinates and, thereby, what is the chain of command. Within the organization there will be sanctions for breaking these 'rules' that are accepted by all within the regime. Acceptance of the rules at the start of a period of employment is a prerequisite to good order and control.

Extreme rules may be imposed on society so that the recalcitrant person may be fined or imprisoned – these rules (laws) are established for good order. The situation within organizations is less severe. An offender may receive a strong rebuke or a notice of dismissal. On the other hand, there may be bonuses or privileges that may be won for extra achievements or initiatives beyond the minimum state which is controlled by the rules.

Design management

One cannot turn to the animal kingdom for neat examples and analysis of the combined term 'design management'. It would appear that the genesis of the term was found in the development of industrialized society. Specializations of old crafts and the emergence of new professions blossomed in the post-Fordist era. Design became intertwined with production, and production itself responded to the expanding needs of consumerism.

Design was associated with invention. An idea was generated and the resultant artefact was designed, developed and constructed. Each design/invention was the product of one mind, sometimes with hundreds of prototypes, until the design flourished as a commercial expression, with public acceptability. Early inventors were characteristically lonely people who jealously guarded their intellectual property; many patented their inventions and died without a mention in technology's history books.

Today, design (and one has to couple this term with 'invention') is a major business undertaken by many people, and as such it has to be 'managed'. Design is applied to unique discoveries as well as cosmetically engineering existing products for market. Design creates value; better design creates more value.

A recent example of the power and influence of design management is the humble potato crisp. Mr Smith (and probably generations before him) found that one potato could be cut into slices, each one millimetre thick, fried in hot oil and sold in bags – 'Smith's Crisps' – each bag containing a small blue bag of salt. Consider the features: low material costs and an ease of production (they could be made by hand or with a simple potato cutter) with the product packed into printed bags that advertised a 'brand name' and which included the table salt considered so essential for healthy living in those days.

Today the same product, the potato crisp, has been developed (designed) by a Belgian company and sold as 'Pringles' to consumers world-wide. The crisp has been developed to be uniform in shape, a range of flavours is available and it is packed in cylindrical boxes, which are easily transported and displayed on supermarket shelves. The product is (almost) the universally known potato crisp; the standardization of the shape, the easily identifiable and attractively packaged box are all the result of 'managed' design – a true case of design creating value.

It would appear, therefore, that any study of design management must include a clear indication of the product (the brief), the motivation of, or the process for, an identification of the client/customer, and the marketing support for the venture.

Design management: its position within the firm

For the purpose of this book, the definition of design management, as coined by Heap (1989), is 'the application of the process of management to the processes of innovation and design'. There is a considerable body of research that examines the dimensions and efficiency of design management. This research has shown that effective design management, although not a general panacea of industry, is a significant contributor to success, deserving a place on the corporate agenda (Cooper and Press 1998).

Design, therefore, should not be considered as a 'bolt on' extra but as a pre-requisite to successful and effective products. The design function should be represented at Board level and recognized for its worth and control, and firmly placed within the management structure of any organization.

Topalian (1989) suggested that:

> Success also requires that executive responsibility for design is assigned formally to a senior manager who is given adequate access to, and backing by the Board. Day-to-day responsibility for individual projects tends to be assigned at appropriate levels in the management hierarchy to ensure sufficient authority without wasting senior management time. All those with responsibility for design should have that fact fleshed out in their job descriptions – not merely stated – and the substance of this responsibility reviewed regularly.

Since 1980, Topalian has spelt out what design management encompasses (Figure 1).

Design as problem solving

One of the more esoteric discussions is about the distinction between an inventor and a designer. There is no space here to develop this argument fully, but a few comments may encourage the reader to explore the discussion further.

It seems that an inventor creates by combining or extending technologies into entirely new spheres. The originators of the electric light bulb, electricity itself, the motor car, computers, all had a vision, an imagination, a self-imposed problem that they were able to solve. Even the humble paperclip was born out of necessity – that of producing something which did not have all of the obvious disadvantages of a sharp pin. The inventor of the most successful paperclip, William Middlebrook, in 1899 invented 'a machine for making wire paperclips' – the clip became commonly known as the Gem paperclip.

Many designers have tried to improve on the Gem paperclip (Petroski 1996), for example Gary Michelson in 1990, who described his paperclip as 'a technological advancement, superior to the prior art'. So Michelson was acknowledging the existence of the original Gem paperclip while accepting the same challenge (to secure two or more sheets of paper together) and producing his own solution. He was therefore designing a paperclip, not inventing one (Figure 2).

The Design Management 'Universe'

The lack of a consensus on what design management encompasses remains a critical obstacle to establishing its credibility as a rigorous business discipline. Attempts to define the discipline in a couple of sentences are futile. Yet it is possible to 'map out' the key issues that should be taken into account in professional practice as follows:

Key issues at the corporate level
- Design responsibility and leadership
- Corporate design philosophy and strategy formulation
- Positioning and 'visibility' of design
- Integration of design within an organization
- Auditing corporate design and design management practices
- Introducing an appropriate design management system and infrastructure
- Degree of centralization in managing design
- Establishing and maintaining corporate design standards
- Environmental dimension of design
- Legal dimension of design
- Design awareness and design management skills development programmes
- Corporate design capability
- Design and the manifestation of corporate identity
- Evaluation of the contribution and impact of design on corporate performance
- Funding design activities.

Key issues at the project level
- The design process and different types of design project
- Formulation of design project proposals and the briefing process
- Selection of design specialists
- Composition and management of 'augmented' design project teams
- Planning and administration of design projects
- Costing design work and drawing up project budgets
- Design research and sources of new investment in design
- Presentation of design recommendations
- Design project documentation and control systems
- Implementation and long-term survival of design solutions
- Evaluation of design projects.

Clearly, there is considerable common ground between the management of design and that of other business disciplines. Nevertheless, success with design and the development of a distinctive competence in managing design result from an enlightened handling of the detailed differences.

1 Key design management issues at the corporate and project levels. © *Alan Topalian (1994)*

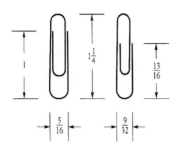

2 Classic Gem paper clip (left) and a recent imitator (dimensions are in inches)

Problem solving is therefore the common link between inventors (those who design something for the first time) and designers, who fashion an artefact within proven technologies. A dress designer, for instance, does not create a new fabric, he or she uses existing materials, albeit in a unique way.

In design situations, the problem is rarely clearly stated at the outset and this phase (of the design process) may require considerable effort (Lawson 1997). The architect/engineer Santiago Calatrava has produced some of the most imaginative and innovative structures of our time, but all in response to specific problems: 'It is the answer to a particular problem that makes the work of the engineer. . . . I can no longer design a pillar or an arch, you know, I need a very precise problem' (Lawson 1994).

A similar statement is attributed to Barnes Wallis: 'There has always been a problem first. I have never had a novel idea in my life. My achievements have been solutions to problems' (Whitfield 1975).

Design can be conceived from being an individual activity, such as designing a chair, to a corporate planning process that regulates innovation to meet market demands. It can be lauded as a model of 'Thatcherite entrepreneurialism' and a willing servant of industry, or as a means of expressing the oppositional values of the punk subculture (Cooper and Press 1998).

It can be argued that designers design solutions (mainly) to other people's problems: a book cover for a publisher, a bridge for other people to use, a toy for somebody else to play with. Architects are rarely promoters or developers, so they too provide a service of creativity focused towards clients' needs. The establishment of a client's brief is the point at which rapid prototyping (Schroge 2000) at the early stage of design 'reduces development time and cost and thus frees up resources to be more innovative in the market place' (Thomke and Tekahiro 1998).

Architectural design management

In the extremely competitive climate of today's construction industry, there is no place for the inefficient or ineffectual business. A company that exposes itself to a higher degree of risk than necessary through lack of in-built protection measures will soon encounter the many pitfalls of this increasingly litigious marketplace. For these reasons, it is becoming ever more important for architectural practices to monitor their management and design procedures to ensure that they reduce risk and remain competitive. In the constantly changing business arena, no company can afford to be complacent or rely on past glories and methods. Constant self-appraisal is essential to ensure that the business remains healthy and there is controlled growth and development.

Design management is a function of all practices, whatever their size, but, as with all specialisms, this function becomes stratified as a specific role within the larger organization.

Management

Management structure

Within the architectural profession and construction industry generally there is a plethora of small firms (i.e. one to ten people). In fact, some 90% of practices fall within this category.

Starting a business may be a simple and quite innocent action, there are (at the time of writing) no legal restrictions to entry to a profession or trade in the UK. Yet, many countries in mainland Europe have a legal requirement of a minimum capital sum as well as minimum professional qualifications. This means that the UK has (and indeed encourages) a lot of people entering into business – it also has a high rate of business closures due, no doubt, to a lack of capital and managerial know how.

At the other end of the scale, the large practices tend to have fairly rigid structures. In one company, the structure is split into six levels of seniority, from director to junior/training level, for each of the different disciplines. Thus, everybody knows their place in the pecking order. Similarly, they are aware that progress through the ranks is possible, indeed it is encouraged.

Management culture

Each firm develops its own culture, usually reflecting the personality of the founding member(s). One architectural practice that has been in existence for some twenty-one years, employing about twenty people, has what it refers to as a 'family attitude to the management of the practice'. As this family culture conflicts with the notion of rigid office procedures, few exist – and as a logical extension, neither written rules nor regulations are significantly in evidence. This family attitude is interesting; it manifests itself within the practice in the following ways:

- The senior staff promote and encourage an informal communication between all levels of staff.
- Staff members take an active and personal interest in each other's welfare, both within and outside office hours.
- The normal office hours are reduced on Fridays so that people either can get home early for the weekend, or can regroup in a bar for a social drink together.
- Birthdays and other significant events are noted and celebrated by all levels of staff.

- The senior partner is known and appreciated for occasionally arriving in the office on a Friday afternoon with several bottles of wine and snacks to share with the staff.

A tremendous affect on morale can be effected on staff by this family attitude. It is particularly noticeable to new staff who get this sense of welcome and well-being – loyalty is immediately established. Such a working relationship allows staff to transfer easily between design teams as the loyalty is to the firm rather than to any (possibly divisive) rigid design-team structure.

There are, of course, dangers in this cosy family approach. Staff may work at the level of the lowest common denominator; there may not be healthy competition within the organization, or a striving for excellence; staff may inadvertently be working outside the cover of the firm's professional indemnity insurance. By contrast with the more *laissez-faire* ethos within practices, there are still many organizations in which the proprietor or managing director will not let go: he or she will not delegate. The nineteenth-century practice of the head of the firm opening and reading all letters before distribution to staff, coupled with the imposition of personally signing all outward correspondence, is still endemic in large firms and departments. This insistence on inspection at high level can only reduce any initiative on the part of an individual, causing frustration, and a strong sense of unease and tension. Even with e-mail communications, some heads of firms have the only e-mail address for the whole practice, so that everything can be scrutinized and challenged.

Rules and regulations within a design office may be disliked by individuals, but their presence is essential as a basis for delegation with control. Teamwork works and is both efficient and effective as opposed to the firm comprising of a set of individuals with no unified sense of direction. Office manuals and quality assurance systems are installed to help and not to restrict the activities of the individual.

Whether a family business or a mega undertaking, all firms have to balance their social and professional activities – each aspect has corporeal benefits within the complexity of a practice. Yet, balance is the key, and so too is the diligence to keep appraising that balance as the practice grows and develops within an evolving social and commercial world.

Managing design

In the 1990s, Alexander Groonewege from The Netherlands was asked by a design manager to make some suggestions for a range of hairdryers that Philips would produce. These products had to compete with Japanese goods (Japan being the current world leaders in this product). The general qualities that Groonewege had to aim for were obvious but, somewhat, contradictory: solid quality, but with fun and personality. The detailing was to be perfect, the design innovative.

Groonewege mused on a number of images. He is quoted (Dormer 1991) as saying: 'Drying your hair you start dreaming about waving palm leaves along Pacific beaches, Spanish Flamenco dancers, Japanese geishas . . . everyone has his owns thoughts.' In reviewing how he developed the image of the hand-held, non-technological fan as the basis for his hairdryer, Groonewege retraced his steps as follows:

- I did not begin with 'form follows function'.
- I started with wind, not with the thing that produces it.
- Then I thought about things that pushed and pulled and floated in the wind – feathers, birds, aeroplanes, wings, palm trees, leaves.
- Put style and wind together and you have peacock.
- A peacock's fantail is like a fan that Spanish women use to wave air. The fan has a lot of hidden tempo to it: rhythm, flamenco, tension and tenderness.
- In my imagination, the step to Japan (a styling and competitive must for my product) was not big.

He did not want his peacock to look like existing versions of hairdryers (Brown or Atlantic Design) because they were too well known and offered no novelty. Groonewege's hairdryer was not another hand-held pistol, but an illusion of fans, to grace and air.

Clearly, the design manager cannot enter the ethereal world of the designer, nor that of the architect, yet some parameters have to be set in order to control (as far as possible) the designer's activities. Gray *et al.* (1994) used RIBA's *Architects' Handbook' – Plan of Work* (1970) 'because it more closely reflects the stages of management needed to achieve a rigorous and disciplined regime of signing off'. They continued: 'It also allows a better understanding of the pattern of contributions to the design and communication systems typical on most projects.'

Such 'artificial' boundaries to the design process would be anathema to such designers and Groonewege, who could not flourish within such a tightly controlled regime. Yet, within the commercial world of architectural design, fees have to be estimated and agreed, timetables and schedules adhered to, deadlines set and met for a firm to survive. This dichotomy between the designer's obvious need for freedom and space and lack of constraints with the design manager's imperative to keep to targets and guarantee costs with profits is a constant source of frustration. A balance has to be found.

> We're both designers and hopeless businessmen. We both make sure there's no profit – you could say that's a pathology we share.
>
> (Edward Jones on his partnership with Sir Jeremy Dixon,
> *The Observer*, 12 March 2000)

Architectural management

In 1962, the RIBA published research findings called *The Architect and His Office*. It was a damning publication that strongly criticized the competence of architectural practices and confessed that it was difficult to see how the mass of small practices making up the profession could be professionally effective or financially viable. Management was criticized as incompetent and unrealistic, calls were made for changes in education, to rules governing the solicitation of work, and to the fee scales. The report commented that

> Management is a word which up to now has been relatively little used in connection with the architect's work and education. . . . It is a word, which frequently evokes strong feelings of hostility and disdain among architects for they see in it the cold hand of logic and calculation descending on the delicate creative mysteries of their art.

The report continued: 'This mistrust is understandable; we have felt it too. Management techniques misapplied can wreak havoc among complex and highly charged relationships of the design group.' Reiterating the arguments of the 1880s, the report stated that the practice of architecture is both a business and an art, therefore possibly benefiting from the management techniques seen in manufacturing industry, the civil service and the armed forces. 'There is no reason why architects should not be rather good at that sort of thing,' it suggested, even though it was added in faintest élitist tones, architectural management would have to function within a group 'operating at a high level of emotion and intelligence'. The report emphasized that

> The architect is still, after all, the one man in the building team who is present in a controlling position at all stages of the work from brief to accounts. . . . It is his presence which must give direction and continuity to the process and unity to the end product. He is thus presented with all the classical management problems in such a way that many sectors look to him to take the initiative in proposing solutions. Ignorance of, or what is worse, hostility towards the field of knowledge which deals precisely with such problems ill becomes the profession which should be in a position of leadership in the building industry.

Reform to the architectural profession in particular and the construction industry in general was the theme of many government reports which began with the Phillips Report of 1950 criticizing the lack of common education for those engaged in design and construction. Twelve years later, the Emmerson Report (1962) and then the Banwell Report (1964) criticized the failure of the building industry to provide an integrated service of design and production. The Tavistock Report (1965) by Higgins and Jessop, *Communications in the Building Industry*, exposed the lack of sound communications within the structure and practices extant in the construction industry (Gruneberg 1995).

During 1993, Sir Michael Latham was commissioned jointly by the Department of the Environment and the construction industry to review the performance of the industry and how it could be improved. The resulting report, *Constructing the Team* (1994) contained around thirty recommendations to reform the construction industry. The report expressed a wish to reduce the confrontational attitude within the construction industry. It also recommended that the previous role of the architect as quasi arbitrator should be replaced by a 'separation of the roles of contract administrator, project or lead manager, and adjudicator. The project or lead manager should be clearly identified as client's representative'.

A further definition of roles within the construction industry was recommended by the Egan Report *Rethinking Construction* (1998) – the report of a task force under the chairmanship of Sir John Egan – which concluded:

> we are asking the industry and Government to join with major clients to do it entirely differently. What we are proposing is a radical change in the way we build. We wish to see, within five years, the construction industry deliver its products to its customers in the same way as the best consumer-led manufacturing and service industries. To achieve the dramatic increases in efficiency and quality that are both possible and necessary, we must all rethink construction.

Now, particularly with the formation of the Clients' Forum, the joint lobby of clients, construction professionals and government, all are conspiring to redefine the architect's role. No longer is the architect, as claimed in the RIBA 1962 report *The Architect and His Office*, 'the one man in the building team who is present in a controlling position at all stages of the works', but the architect is integrated within the supply side of construction, particularly in the large contracts. Where the architect is expected to offer a 'full service' is in the plethora of small contracts for what Higgins and Jessop (1965) refer to as naïve clients.

What does the architect expect to do for a commission? According to the Standard Form of Architect's Appointment (RIBA 1990), the architect 'Assists clients at all stages of a building project and co-ordinates all the elements of design and construction process.' It further states, 'The Architect's primary professional responsibility is to act as the client's advisor and additionally, administer the building contract fairly between client and contractor.' Therefore, the architect is largely a coordinator of the design and construction processes.

As early as 1872 (and probably earlier), the members of the RIBA were governed by the Charters, Bylaws and Code of Professional Conduct of the Royal Institute (RIBA 1872). The Conditions of Engagement in 1872 referred to periodic supervision and inspection of the works by the architect, his authority to give orders on behalf of the client, his duty to provide 'as built' drawings and the engagement of consultants to be approved by the architect and appointed and paid by the client. These duties are similarly described today, although the term 'supervision' has been dropped in favour of the contractor. The authority to give orders, in other words to act as agent for the client, is now embedded in the standard form of building contract between the employer and the contractor.

It is useful to look back to the Simon Report (1944), particularly about the role of the architect in supervision. In the report, terms were being used (and presumably were commonly accepted) such as 'the erection of a building is controlled by an architect on behalf of the owner' and 'he [the architect] may in his absolute discretion give the contractor instructions . . .'. Each party in the construction and design processes knew their roles (players in the game) and still the communications between the parties and the coordination of their several parts were under scrutiny.

The full services of the architect in building design was described (in 1872) as follows:

> For taking the Clients' instructions, preparing sketch designs, making appropriate estimate by cost by cubic measurement or otherwise, submitting applications for building or other licences and town planning, bye-law or other approvals, preparing working drawings, specifications or such particulars as may be necessary for the preparation of bills of quantities by an independent Quantity Surveyor, or for the purpose of obtaining tenders, advising on tenders and preparation of contract, nominating and instructing Consultants (if any) preparing, and supplying for the use of the Contractor, two copies of all drawings, specification or other particulars and of such further details as are necessary for the proper carrying out of the works, giving general supervision as defined in the Conditions of Engagement (RIBA, 1872 p. 1), issuing certificates for payment, and certifying accounts. . . .

One might expect the conditions to have stated that the architect actually designs the building, yet this basic truth is not spelled out in simple terms. It may come as a surprise to many non-architect designers to find that their common-law liability for design is more onerous than that imposed by the RIBA conditions which warrant only that the designer is a reasonably competent person and that he will exercise the skill of a reasonably competent designer (Toole 1990). It should be noted that in addition to the defined processes of the design work, the architect took responsibility for the following activities, all of which were clearly managerial roles:

* Making an approximate estimates of costs
* Advising on tenders
* Preparing the contract
* Instructing consultants
* Site supervision
* Issuing certificates
* Certifying accounts.

The architect is to act as adviser to the client; in this, he clearly has a professional responsibility. His knowledge of the design and construction process must be adequate and sufficiently specialized in order that the architect is in a position to offer advice to the client. The architect has to be the administrator of the contract between the two parties to the building contract – the client and the contractor. In this role, architects act as quasi arbitrators who are frequently put into the invidious position of making a judgement against the very person who is their client and paymaster.

It is within this confused and perhaps obscure basis of engagement that many architects have recently explored other routes of procurement; other forms of contract; other constructional techniques; and other non-standard methods of providing services. Forward-thinking architects, clients and contractors who have experimented with many systems have now eroded the 'traditional' route, and some of these systems will be explored here.

Variety of procurement routes

The procurement of design services is inextricably entwined with the organizational management of the construction process and the division of roles and responsibilities. At the most basic level, the architect may offer his or her services to produce a design for a building and have no further interest or involvement with that building. This service may be offered to a private client or a builder client, either of whom will take over the responsibility for the production of the building, using the architect's design.

In 1983, the British Property Federation (BPF) produced its solution to the 'traditional' methods of procurement and management in the form of a manual (BPF 1983). Being representative of the largest property owners and developers in the UK, the BPF was able to influence matters in a more demonstrative way than any previous body, including the government. In his Introduction, the President of the BPF wrote:

> To build in this country costs too much, takes too long and does not always produce creditable results. . . . The purpose of this manual is not to tell other people their business; it does not seek to prescribe how architects, contractors or other professionals should perform the specialist work in which they are the trained experts. Nor does it seek to blame everyone but the client for the present unsatisfactory state of affairs. We all share responsibility for the status quo, and we all need to co-operate in the cure.

The BPF system introduced for the first time the notion of a technical client's representative (who may or may not be an architect), a design leader (to coordinate the design processes) and a separate supervisor (who again, may or may not be an architect) to maintain the standards of the contractor. Design activities were not confused by other responsibilities and the coordination role was to be undertaken by a separate design leader. The client's representative appointed all parties with separate contracts between themselves and the client. This stripped the architect of his or her advisory, coordination, supervisory and arbitral roles that were the buttresses of the Standard Conditions of Engagement.

Whilst the BPF and others have actively developed new procurement routes and new definitions of roles, the RIBA has commented through Dr Francis Duffy (RIBA 1995b), who wrote in his Introduction to the *Strategic Study*,

> I believe it has been (a) twenty year failure of confidence, this freezing of our collective imaginative faculty – that explains why architects have been so slow to

change our ways of thinking and working in response to what is clearly a totally different, and in many ways much more challenging environment.

Project management and construction management techniques (Franks 1984) are still undergoing development, as are the earlier management fee systems. Each of these methods virtually excludes the architect from his or her duties beyond the design of the building. The contractor (or manager) has a direct contractual relationship with the client and is treated as an equal professional with architects and others. The responsibility for design and production is again distanced. Management contracts have recently suffered from considerable criticism from clients who expressed dismay over the lack of control over the final costs. Some clients forecast a growth in construction management, probably in the hands of a limited number of large contractors.

Design and build

Design and build market

A study of the design and build market (Centre for Construction Market Information 1987) showed that architects, clients and contractors all expected the size of the market to increase substantially in the following five years. A study was conducted by the Centre for Construction Market Information (CCMI) and was sponsored by the RIBA through the Client's Advisory Service and several leading contractors. On the basis of the answers received from architects, clients and contractors involved in design and build, and an examination of the recent contracts, CCMI estimated that the total value of the non-housing design and build market was about £1,500 million during 1986. This was over 20% of the total non-housing new build market. It also expected a growth rate of 18% for 1987.

Of the respondent architectural practices with experience of design and build, 80% had eleven or more architectural staff. During 1986, 73% of the practices that had used the design-and-build approach stated that it accounted for less than 25% of their total workload by value. The vast majority of practices (88%) expected the contractor's market for design and build to increase in the next three years. In the period after that, 59% of practices expected the market to expand. Seventy-seven per cent of practices thought that the amount of design and build work for the whole architectural profession would increase after 1987.

The report's analysis of design-and-build projects provided an insight into the structure of the market with important implications for the architectural and fee-bidding profession, in particular the increasing role of the contractor rather than the architect in the initiation of projects. During 1986, of the overall value of non-housing design and build work, about 10% involved refurbishment and 27% was carried out for the public sector. Sixty per cent of the projects analysed went to a one-stage bid, with 26% being negotiated and 14% proceeding to two-stage bids. Furthermore, 77% of projects involved lump sum prices. The client's internal department initiated most of the projects (63%). Contractors and surveyors were each responsible for initiating 18% of the projects. In only 4% of cases did architects initiate the use of a design and build solution. There is a clear message for the architectural profession here. Either it views design and build as a serious option for certain building projects or it risks losing out to other suppliers of services in the industry in what is a growing sector of the market.

The selection of the architect at the concept stage was divided in this report between the contractor's choice (47%), contractor's in-house architects (30%) and the client (22%). However, at the detailed drawing stage, 70% of the architects were the contractor's in-house employees, with 16% being the contractor's external choice of consultant and 11% the client's external selection. However, these projects were selected by the contractors themselves and may have been distorted by their choice of sample.

The average value of the design-and-build projects examined was £2.75 million, with 37% of the projects being worth between £1 million and £5 million. This compares with the average contract value for all building work of approximately £220,000. Although there may have been an element of bias in the respondents' selection of contracts, it appears that the average design and build contract is worth considerably more than the average building contract.

Perhaps the most interesting finding was that at the outline design stage, 41% of architects said that they worked on a 'no job, no fee basis'. At the detailed design stage, the proportion was 16%. The CCMI concluded that 'It is apparent that the architect is subject to a fairly high risk element.' It based this conclusion on the fact that in one in five cases, the practice risked receiving no fee even though a considerable amount of work may have been carried out. The figures provided by the clients were even more emphatic. At the outline stage, 82% of projects were conducted on a no job, no fee basis. At the detailed design stage, 68% of tenders were on a no job, no fee basis. The CCMI stated that 'Even at the full design stage a staggering 81% of tenders were submitted on a "no job, no fee basis", illustrating the enormous risk to the architect if the proposal should fail.' Obviously, the degree of risk associated with tendering for a design-and-build project is great and not all practices can tolerate such a high probability of failure.

Practices tendering for design and build contracts need to ensure that they are geared up for and have a 'balanced portfolio of risk' across the whole range of their work to ensure the tenders that are more likely to fail are counterbalanced by bids that have a higher chance of success. Architectural practices in the CCMI survey were also asked about their views on the advantages and disadvantages of the design-and-build approach to the client. There was more of a consensus concerning the advantages: 46% of practices felt that design and build improved the speed of the project and led to completion on time. Forty-nine per cent of respondents also felt that design and build benefited the client because it established a single point of contact. There was less unanimity of view about the disadvantages to clients. Twenty-nine per cent of architects thought that design and build led to poor design and building standards. Twenty per cent also felt that such an approach meant that the client lacked independent advice. The architects' views about the advantages of design and build to the client were very similar to those expressed by both contractors and clients. On the other hand, architects perceived considerably more disadvantages to the client from using a design-and-build approach than did the contractors or the clients themselves.

There was a considerable variation between the forms of engagement practices normally had with design-and-build contractors. The two most frequently cited were 'letters of appointment' (34%) and 'amended standard forms of agreement' (29%). The number of other forms of engagements listed by practices provided the distinct impression that practices were approaching this issue in an ad-hoc manner. This view was reinforced by practices' answers to questions concerning their relationships with contractors and what defined responsibility practices normally had for work on site. The CCMI summarized its findings in this section by commenting: 'Some of the answers were related to answers on forms of engagement, but in general answers on both engagement and responsibility were very vague – to an extent that might be considered surprising if not disquieting.' Fully, 44% of practices carrying out design and build said that their responsibility to the contractor was normally only 'vague or not defined' – only 20% said that they normally had some form of contract arrangement.

Design and build has been a clear winner of the late 1980s' construction boom, according to what is probably the most comprehensive investigation of UK construction procurement. The CCMI survey revealed a parallel growth in design and build and in management contracting. However, while most clients, architects and contractors were confident about the continued rise of design and build, they were less optimistic about the future for management contracting.

Analysis of nearly 9,000 projects on a contract databank, validity checks, interviews and a telephone survey of 150 specific projects were among approaches adopted by the CCMI to arrive at market estimates. All building and civil engineering sectors were covered. In 1989, 15.5% (£5,568 million) of all new construction orders were specified design and build. Non-housing orders accounted for £4,455 million of that, compared with £1,322 million three years earlier. In 1989, after civil engineering was stripped out, design and build took a 17% share of commercial projects and 22% of the industrial sector.

The RIBA (1995b) *Strategic Study* when discussing building trends in the Higher Education Sector, reported the following comments from clients:

Design and Build will continue to dominate the procurement of
accommodation;
Older universities are more likely to favour traditional, architect-led
procurement while newer universities are more likely to favour design and build;
Virtually all our building is Design and Build;
We haven't used Design and Build extensively to date, but we'll have to take it
more seriously.

Management contracts (Figure 3), including construction management, have witnessed considerable growth. They took a 14.8% share by value (£5,316 million) of all orders in 1989, with management contracting believed to have captured at least 90% of that share. The average value of a 1989 management contract was £12 million. A few years ago, the CCMI found that design and build and management contracting had a 10–12% share of the non-housing market. However, there was a stark contrast in the number of contractors offering the two services. There are now 495 firms practising design and build; in 1986 there were just 150.

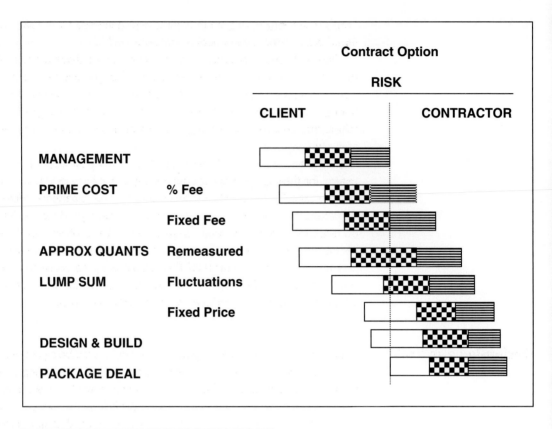

3 Contract options and the division of risk between clients and contractors. *Source: Clamp (1993)*

The number using management contracting has levelled off; in 1986, there were 46, whereas at the date of publication there are 57.

One of the most revealing statistics concerned the shape of the construction market in two years' time. Asked if they thought design and build would increase its share, 48% more clients, contractors and architects answered 'yes' than 'no'. A majority of 12% thought management contracting would continue to win new business and, among contractors, it gained an even more marginal majority.

Design-and-build projects are praised for keeping to budget and, to a lesser extent, for their speed. Repeat business is growing since design and build's success, says the CCMI report. 'It is based on trust and experience.' However, only the contractors believe that this procurement route produces better-designed buildings. Architects and clients disagree. Part of the problem, says the CCMI, is the lack of guidance available to clients on how to commission design-and-build projects and provide a clear brief. The Centre identified the same problem four years previously and urged the RIBA to draft a guide, but the report says that 'Nothing has been done and the complaint is still widespread.'

Design-led and build

Possibly realizing that work, responsibilities and fees are being eroded from the architect in his or her traditional role, some architects are acting as lead consultants and contractors. They take the initiative and gain the commissions directly from the client, and in addition to providing a full design service, they 'employ' the contractor. The benefits of design and build as one package have always appealed to the clients who wanted one point of contact with the building team. The process, therefore, can work equally well whether the architect or the builder is taking the lead. The possible weakness of this system is that if the architect 'employs' the builder, he or she is taking on an excessive level of risk should his contractor fail to perform.

Domus Design Build's founder and Managing Director, Mike Duckering, is one architect who joined the fray and is now coordinating the aims of design, surveying engineering and construction staff (Evemy 1990). Many other design-and-build firms are prospering at the expense of the 'traditional' firms. The simplification of communication routes leads to faster design times and a joint commitment to design and build as quickly as possible. The system may be 'contractor led' or 'design led' depending on the expertise and aspirations of the joint participants. There is also benefit in a more industrial capital structure and an advantage in limited liability.

It has taken some 150 years for the construction professions to become closer to one another. The separation of disciplines caused jealousies and protectionism, each party faced the other in a litigious stance ready for immediate combat. The nineteenth-century documents (RIBA 1872) confirm that architects took responsibility for financial advice, cost estimates and such like. This position still pertains today, together with the architect's responsibility for advising the client and coordinating the design and construction processes. However, this element of practice has come under severe criticism. Schneider and Davies (1995) said that 'The architect as a "brand" has become tarnished, and less and less a source of added value.' They continued:

> The service provided by architects was disappointing to most of those (20 clients) interviewed. Reflecting the profession's perceived failure to manage time and money, the study also highlighted how architects have been ousted from an 'upstream' position of client's adviser, 'friend' and team leader, to that of a 'downstream' supplier – one of many.

Modern methods of procurement and contractual responsibilities are eroding these traditional foundations of the architect's role within the construction industry.

Management contracts, the BPF system, design and build are all systems that help to remove the adversarial positions of professionals. The leaders of the team are not automatically architects, but the person (or firm) best suited to the challenges of the particular job.

Much of the decision-making in the building procurement process takes place in the environment within which the objectives, constraints and consequences of possible actions are not known precisely (Bellman and Zadeh 1970). In the construction context, uncertainty and risk are evidenced as soon as the client decides to proceed with the construction project. Although the potential client may have a general idea of his or her requirements, the details of the brief mature as he or she gathers expertise from advisers and later as the designs are implemented from the drawings and models.

Division of risks

The following seeks to analyse the division of risks that are apportioned to various consultants and contractors in the construction process using the design-and-build method of procurement as a basis for discussion.

According to Mandani and Efstathiou (1985), no one technique exists that is capable of facilitating the treatment of the variety of different forms of uncertainty (and risk) described by Fox (1986). Classifications of the various types of uncertainty have been compiled and such a philosophy has already been proposed within the property valuation context (Erwin et al. 1991):

- Imperfect knowledge: may be poor brief taking or standards.
- Intensive randomness, e.g. if a building was over a certain height it would probably need a reinforced concrete frame.
- Inherent indeterminacy: such as the dampness inside the wall may be caused by a burst pipe, ground water or condensation.
- Categorical uncertainty: often items of quality and finish – a 'luxurious finish' is required of the 'best possible standard'.

Many of these types of uncertainty appear in contract documents because decisions relating to these items have not yet been taken. It is not known, for example, how many site meetings will yet be held because the cost of attendance at the meetings has to be estimated by the architects and consultants before the job has started. The risk, therefore, in bidding for fees has to be calculated on an assumption of the proposed length of the job and the probable number of meetings each week or month.

The uncertainty of various types exists at all stages of the building contract and procurement processes and may be explained as either uncertainty of outcome or as uncertainty of explanation. The risks associated with these uncertainties are apportioned within the forms of agreements in various contracts and may or may not be evenly distributed between the parties.

In the changing competitive business environment today, clients are under pressure to accelerate project delivery (Kwakye 1991a). The traditional sequential mode of construction procurement has failed to respond to the accelerating changes in the business environment and clients' demands are not being met. For this reason, non-traditional methods of procurement are being sought by clients and adopted by building contracting companies.

Design followed by construction has always been considered as the 'traditional route' and many methods of procurement have been devised to phase the construction so that it overlaps the design process. The most successful method that achieves this aim is fast tracking (Kwakye 1991b). It was designed to increase the rate at which a project can be built. The restriction of fast tracking is that it is based on the premise that the separate functions of designing and building are carried out by different disciplines in unrelated organizations. This need not necessarily be true, for as Deming (1986) wrote, 'Efficient processes are those which are uninterrupted.' 'Interruptions cause a break in the flow of activity' (Gray 1994). 'Where a process is divided and uncertain, so it becomes more complex to identify and consequently, difficult to manage.' Where the designing and building are part of one uninterrupted process within one organization, fast tracking will naturally occur.

The design and build method can be considered as a form of fast tracking (Figure 4). This system brings together the two main elements of the building construction management, even if they are still carried out by separate firms. The communication between designers and constructors is immediate and not cluttered by separate (sometimes conflicting) contractual responsibilities.

It is this immediacy and openness of communication that is the main feature of design and build. The expertise of the contractor in areas such as buildability, the availability of materials, the ability to purchase goods and services, together with a fundamental experience in project management are elements that make design and build so attractive to clients, architects and builders alike.

There is an occasional advantage of design and build in that if the sector of the market is restricted, it is possible for the client to visit a building with similarities to his or her own needs already completed by the organization. If this is contrived during briefing, then there are considerable benefits to be gained by all concerned. In the traditional form of procurement, this occurs only if the architect specializes in a building type, as in schools, religious buildings, etc. Few practices

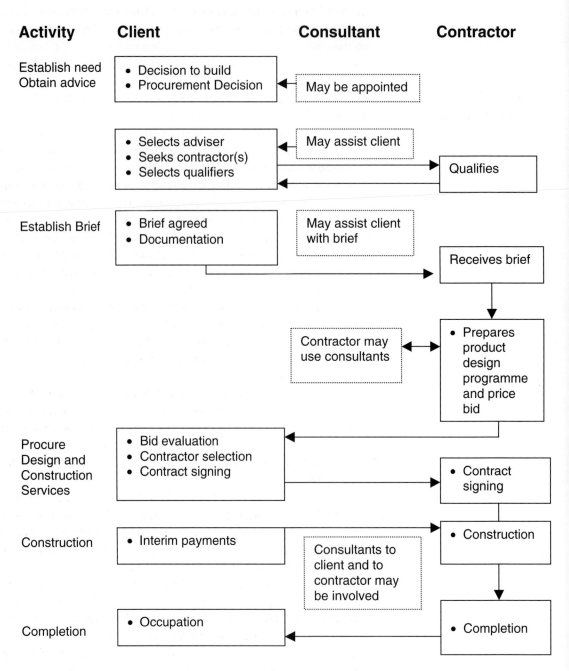

Activity	Client	Consultant	Contractor
Establish need Obtain advice	• Decision to build • Procurement Decision	May be appointed	
	• Selects adviser • Seeks contractor(s) • Selects qualifiers	May assist client	Qualifies
Establish Brief	• Brief agreed • Documentation	May assist client with brief	Receives brief
		Contractor may use consultants	• Prepares product design programme and price bid
Procure Design and Construction Services	• Bid evaluation • Contractor selection • Contract signing		• Contract signing
Construction	• Interim payments	Consultants to client and to contractor may be involved	• Construction
Completion	• Occupation		• Completion

4 Components of the design-
and-build system

can focus their work to such an extent and have a continuity of commissions. On the other hand, a preferred form of construction can be promoted and adapted to many uses.

Risks and responsibilities

The separate duties of the architect were set out clearly by the Ministry of Works in 1944:

> The architect has full responsibility for the preparation of the contract and is indeed in sole control until it is signed. When work begins on site the architect is responsible for seeing that the contractor carries out the work in every respect in accordance with the contract and to his reasonable satisfaction. What design and build does is to remove all of this responsibility and shift it to the contractor. The architect does not have control of the entire range of decisions before a contract is signed and does not take any responsibility for supervision. What the architect undertakes is to 'exercise reasonable skill and care in conformity with the normal standards of the architects' profession'. Furthermore, (in most contracts) he agrees to use all reasonable endeavours to perform the design services so as not to hinder or impede the timeous completion of the works as a whole and shall proceed with the design services with all reasonable diligence as circumstances shall allow.

The usual contracts also bind the architect to work to the contractor's programme even if the programme is amended – thus imposing a risk of the unknown onto the designers. The line of communication is also made clear in the contract between the architect and the contractor. This frequently strips the architect of his or her position as leader of the design process and as consultant to the client.

By tradition, the architect's role has always been to coordinate the design function (RIBA 1982). Clause 3.7 of the standard Architect's Appointment clearly states: 'The architect will have the authority to co-ordinate and integrate into the overall design the services provided by any consultant, however employed.' The design–build contracts frequently refer to the coordination role of the contractor (Wimpey Construction UK 1990): 'The Contractor shall be responsible for all co-ordination of design whether from the architect, other consultants or other sub-contractors and whether relating to co-ordination on or off the site.' Where the architect takes a heavy risk is in the event of termination of the contract. In Clauses 7.5 and 7.6 (Wimpey Construction UK 1990), it states: 'If the contract is terminated [the contract between the contractor and the client] for any reason, this agreement shall terminate *ipso facto*. [Furthermore], this agreement may be terminated at any stage by the contractor giving 14 days' notice in writing to the architect.' The implications of these clauses do not encourage considerable forward planning on the part of the architect as his or her work may be terminated at any time.

One clause in the Wimpey contract that must have emanated from bitter past experience is under the Schedule for Design Services. Clause 1.3 states: 'Consider parameters for noise levels in respect of noise emanating from the completed works or noise created externally from any source which may affect the design of the works, and is reasonably apparent at the time.'

Probably the most contradictory clause in the Wimpey document is under the Schedule for Design Services, Clause 1.7: 'Liaise with other consultants and specialist sub-contractors if appointed by the contractor.' One may ask, does this negate all previous clauses relating to coordination, or is it possible to liaise but not to coordinate?

Design-and-build methods are increasing in their use and acceptance in both the UK and USA. Denning (1992) and Summitters (1992) attest to the advancement of design and build in the USA, while Ndekugri and Turner (1994) have studied its growth in the UK. It appears that successes in the private sector markets have encouraged public commitment, particularly when increased quality and cost effectiveness have been demonstrated.

Songer and Ibbs (1995) identified the difficulty of determining an appropriate balance between innovation in design and net construction techniques and the levels of control or freedom in design-and-build situations. What is particularly interesting is that they studied this from the viewpoint of the public-sector client. When the research is completed, this may encourage more public-sector agencies to promote design and build whilst retaining their exposure to public scrutiny and accountability.

Contracts in current use

In a survey recently undertaken by the author, respondents were asked which type of contract they regularly used. Subsequent forms have superseded the standard forms of contract between architects and their clients; the Architect's Appointment was superseded by the Standard Form of Agreement in 1992 and more recently the Conditions of Engagement in 1995 and Standard Form of Agreement SFA/99 (RIBA 1999d). With the exception of the smallest category of practice (Figure 5), all firms are still using the old Architect's Appointment. Still important is the SFA/92 (RIBA 1992), at the expense of CE/95 (RIBA 1995a) and SFA/99. Further research will show how quickly the architectural profession adopts the latest form of contract. The current position would not indicate a rush towards the later forms.

Prominent in the survey was the use of letters as instruments of contract. For the smallest firms (no employees), letters were the only documentation of contract, implying a possible reluctance to use standard forms. Practices employing between one and ten technical staff and those employing between twenty-one and fifty staff all had their own forms of contract. The survey overall showed a reluctance to use any standard forms of contract; they rather tended towards own contracts, letters, verbal agreements or even the 'handshake.'

Owing to the plethora of forms of contract between designers and constructors currently in use, each form of contract has to be scrutinized and the

Size of Firm

Handshake	
Verbal	
Own contract	
Letter	
CE 95	
SFA 92 + SFA 99	
Architect's Appointment	

5 Architects' contracts with clients by size of the practice

balance of risk assessed. It seems clear that most non-standard forms of contract are contractor-driven and, consequently, tend to be biased in their favour. On the other hand, the architect has lost his responsibility for costs, time and the quality of the work. His or her duties have been reduced in some contracts to the design process, without even the responsibility for the coordination of specialist inputs into that design.

Brooks method of architect selection

In the Introduction to the 'Brooks Method', the (then) Director General of the RIBA, Alexander Reid, declared: 'Competition for building is a disease which is striking at the heart of British architecture.' He further suggested that fee competition was the excuse for second-rate buildings and the cause of demise in education, training and technology (Bennett and Jayes 1995).

The Brooks Method (Hamilton 1995) entails seven procedural stages for procurement of architectural services: advertisement, submissions, review of submissions, quality ranking of respondents, interviews/discussions, negotiation and engagement. Fees come into the discussions only when quality ranking has been established.

The US Brooks Act 1972 enforced as a matter of public policy 'to negotiate contacts for architectural and engineering services on the basis of demonstrated competence and qualification for the type of professional services required at fair and reasonable prices.'

A subsequent publication, based on the Brooks Act 1972, published jointly by the Construction Industry Council (CIC) and the RIBA (1999c), *Engaging an Architect: Guidance for Clients to Quality-based Selection* (QBS), develops the earlier

Brooks Method. It proposes the key selection criteria by QBS for consultants to be:

- Qualifications
- Experience
- Ability
- Integrity.

This twenty-three-page document guides clients through the three steps for selection, definition and appointment. It concludes weighting proposals for use in quality evaluation, with analysis for group interview analysis.

Bids and fees

To bid or not to bid

A classic argument against bidding is promoted by many members of the architectural profession. It is argued that competitive bidding reduces prices to levels that inhibit good design. This line of reasoning suggests that the design process is intuitive and needs time in which to flourish and develop. Fixing an artificial time limit on the creative process, it is argued, can only result in poorly designed buildings, which cannot give pleasure either to the owner or to the designer. However, it is these same architects who will support the use of profession-wide fee scales so that competition is based on merit and not price.

Bidding has been variously described as guesswork, shots in the dark, a gamble or a lottery. Clearly, the cost of any service cannot be truly known until the task has been completed. Yet clients rarely have unlimited funds with which to satisfy an indulgent designer. Philanthropic patrons of the arts are scarcely to be found in modern society. It is the clients who are demanding firm estimates of the works, whether they are for the designer, the production processes or a combination of the two. Clients are thereby shifting the risk from themselves (by offering an open chequebook) to the designer (who guarantees a firm quotation for the work). Clients are not so likely to follow a simple appointment procedure such as taking soundings and choosing an architect on the basis of trusted advice (Symes *et al.* 1995). They are now more likely to run a complex selection process comparing a range of possible design teams. Fee bids have become an important feature. They did not exist previously and can now take 10–20% of a senior staff member's time. The relationship between client and architect is far less one of gentlemanly trust than it used to be. As someone recently commented, 'as soon as one is no longer treated as a gentleman to be trusted, one ceases to behave as such'. Traditional procurement is still the most popular method of procurement (*Building Design* 1995).

Sawczuk (1996) argued that risk should be identified and addressed. The solution (he suggests) could be to take out innovative design or increase the construction period, or even to change the location of the project. Furthermore, risk can be transferred by a change in procurement method or by taking out insurance cover.

> Estimating for fees is to 'guess' a figure for the work, which will be acceptable to the client, lower than one's competitors, and adequate to cover the required

resources whilst returning a profit. It is very much a balancing act between all of these elements; to consider any one item and to disregard another, will spell disaster. Too high a bid may lose the commission whilst too low a bid will create financial losses and commercial failure. One needs therefore to consider the estimation process as a risk calculation or a determination of the 'odds'.

The basic concept of risk analysis is to reduce each element down to items that can be understood rather than taking a global view of the problem. Take, for example, a passing flock of birds. To look at the sky and state with any accuracy the number of birds in the flock can only be done with prior knowledge or experience. In reality, one would count, say, twenty birds as a group and then estimate the number of groups in the total flock, thus providing a realistic estimate of the total number of birds. So it is with risk. One only has to consider the enormous errors in estimating the cost of megaprojects such as the Aswan Dam or the Channel Tunnel, which were totally outside the comprehension of previous human experience. The final costs escalated to several times the original budgets.

Basis for bidding

According to the Government's Procurement Guide (HM Treasury 1997), there are three principal ways of paying for profession services (sometimes used in combination):

- Time charge
- Lump sum
- *Ad valorem.*

The fee structure to be adopted for the contract will depend on the degree of certainty in the scope and content of the services required. When the scope and content of the services are uncertain, e.g. during the appraisal of options, then reimbursement on a time charge basis is appropriate.

Lump sum charges should only be used where the scope of all the services is defined precisely and there is little risk of significant variations in the scope of the works. A combination of lump sum charges for the more certain elements of the work and time charges for those less certain may offer best value for money (VFM).

Ad valorem fee structures reimburse consultants in proportion (generally as a percentage) to the cost of the project. They appear to provide an incentive for consultants to design expensive projects rather than those offering best VFM.

Call-off arrangements allow a consultant or contractor to be appointed where the precise extent of the work or its duration cannot be determined in advance. Call-off contracts can be based on time charges or on lump sums for specific elements of work. There are particularly useful for the appointment of the client adviser, and value management, risk management and the partnering facilitator. For example, organizations providing value-management services may provide a lump sum for running a value-management study. The bid basis adopted should be that offering the best VFM for the particular project.

Professional indemnity insurance

Professional indemnity (PI) insurance provides cover for the professionals against the financial aspects of legal liability to the client for professional negligence. It is required for all professional appointments, but is costly and may need to be maintained by the consultant for up to 15 years after completion of the contract. The specified levels of cover should appropriate to the particular project. The full cost of requiring an unusually high level of cover should be evaluated before such a requirement is made.

Fee tendering by architects

The formation of the RIBA in 1835 from the joining of groups of provincial societies of architects allowed for the first time the promotion of national agreements of conditions and fees for architect services. The conditions of engagement were enshrined in the RIBA *Conditions of Engagement and Scale of Professional Charges* (1872), which on page 20 defined the architect's services.

It appears from the earliest available records that architects charged a fee based on the final value of the builder's account for his work. Their fees were charged on a scale of fees that related to the complexity and final cost of the building. This meant that the estimation of design fees had to be based on a further estimation of the proposed building costs – which were only 'guesses' at this stage: the two were inextricably entwined.

The establishment of a mandatory fee must have impressed and comforted clients and the public at large because the fees for professional services were the same, countrywide. It must also have helped to allay the fears of corruption and remove the tarnish from the architect's (well-established) image (Beer 1919, Houldsworth 1983).

The percentage fees were well established by 1971, and in subsequent editions of the RIBA's *Conditions of Engagement*, including *The Architect's Appointment* (1982), which stated: 'The recommended fee scales included in this document are based on a percentage of the total construction cost. The RIBA considers these fee scales to be fair and reasonable.' The document then continued to offer definitions of work content for services by reference to the RIBA *Plan of Work* (Stages A–L) (1973) and listed 'other services' that could be offered to the client. In the 1982 document (and CE/95) the fee scales for new works and also for work to existing buildings are displayed in two logarithmic graphs (see Figures 14 and 15, page 76).

Following the RIBA Council's abolition of mandatory fee scales in 1980 and the change of the Code of Contract (1982), the new form only recommended the scale of fees. However, such pressure had been placed on the RIBA by outside agencies that a much revised document, the *Standard Form of Agreement for the Appointment of an Architect* (SFA/92) was approved by the RIBA Council in 1991 and published in 1992. The SFA/92 has two main features: first, it lists in some detail the services that may be required of an architect; second, it does not publish the fee scales. In fact, SFA/92, CE/95, CE/99 (RIBA 1999b) and SFA/99 are singularly quiet on the matter of fee calculation. For the first time since 1895, when a statement of fees relating to specific tasks (in guineas) was published, there was no point of reference within the contract for British architects regarding their fees for professional services. Yet, alongside the forms of contract between the architect and his client, the RIBA has published a series of guides to assist both partners to negotiate fees.

The changes to the RIBA Code in 1980 were seen as the best way of putting architectural practices on a more competitive footing in the new, thrusting commercial world they now inhabited. The extension to this commercializing tendency was that if architects had decided to 'stop viewing themselves as austerely principled Masters of the Universe' (*Architect's Journal* 1995), it would be unsurprising 'if, within a few years, clients began to view them as sub-ontractors in the great chain of construction'. This was echoed by the RIBA (1995b) *Strategic Study* in its discussions with the representatives of Housing Associations who said 'Competitive tendering brought architects off their pedestals.' The vacuum left after the removal of fee-scale graphs caused considerable consternation within the profession, to the point where the RIBA did a complete U-turn and republished the charts in 1994, describing them as 'indicative'. The architectural profession again had its 'prop', and again considered fees as the generators for tendering rather than as the final result of their own calculations (Table 1).

Table 1

Date	Title	New (building) works	Fee (%)
1985	Architects' appointment	base of £20,000 building cost	10.56
1990	Architects' appointment	base of £20,000 building cost	11.38
1994	Engaging an architect: guidance for clients on fees	base of £20,000 building cost	11.38
1996	Architects' services: small works (up to £100,000)	base of £20,000 building cost	11.25
1999	Clients' guide to engaging an architect including guidance on fees	base of £20,000 building cost	12.25

By the mid-1990s, fee bidding became one mode of obtaining work. Remarkably low bids such as the Knightsbridge Courts refurbishment caused Ray Cecil to write in 1992 (*Architect's Journal* 1995):

> Every practitioner who quotes excessively low fees has a ready excuse and justification — most usually that they need the job simply to survive and if they don't offer those fees, another firm will. . . . They are fooling themselves while they betray society, their clients, their colleagues and the principles of professionalism.

It appears that the London practice RMJM had submitted a bid for between 1.24 and 1.74%, when the old rate on the now advisory fee scale would have been 7%.

The following year (1993), Hunt Thompson (*Architect's Journal* 1995) displayed widespread professional anger at the report of their making a zero fee bid for housing regeneration work at the Angell Town estate in Lambeth. Partner Bernard Hunt declared: 'we are not going to break the law, we are not going to sacrifice our integrity. But when it comes to commercial work, don't be surprised when we compete'. Cecil (*Architect's Journal* 1995) pointed out: 'Hunt Thompson has discovered a novel way of avoiding the possibility of being sued for breach of contract. By tendering a nil fee for the options study on the Angell Town Estate, its appointment will be unenforceable, lacking the necessary contractual component of "consideration."' He then went on grimly to lambaste Hunt's activities as being against the interests of the profession as a whole.

After the nationally agreed basis for fee calculation had been abolished, it was the 'silly season' for architects' fee bids. Established practices could refer back to their scant cost records of previous jobs and by using those charts as 'benchmarks' estimate fees for similar work. Young practices without track records or the many established practices that had not invested in sophisticated costing systems, however, were all at sea. Their estimates of fees were little more than guesswork, with one eye on the remaining copies of the then obsolete scales of fees. There was no profession-wide tradition of fee calculation, no experience of 'tendering techniques' (RIBA 1986).

The architectural profession had come a long way since 1747 when it is said (Campbell 1747, p. 155) that architects (who may have been master tradesmen) were responsible for the production process and the hiring and firing of tradesmen and labourers, or even to build for a fixed price. (Architect-led design and build?) From being at the heart of the building process, architects had become observers of an activity regarding the day-to-day realities of prices and costs of construction. What was more worrying, they were not sure of their own costs for the design and supervision elements.

According to Ogunlana (1989), not only architects, but also construction work generally suffers the effects of uncertainty more than most human undertakings, and construction cost estimating is perhaps the most error-prone activity in construction. He argued further that cost estimating was error-prone for two reasons. First, it depended on historical cost data; in construction work, history has a rather unusual tendency of not repeating itself. Second, cost estimating attempts to predict future human actions in a world where things are never static. The result has been that the accuracy achieved in estimating has been less than desirable and by chance high bids generally compensate for accidental low bids (Ashworth and Skitmore 1982).

The effects of over- and underestimating have been illustrated in the 'Freiman Curve' (Figure 6). Classic inaccuracies in estimating abound within the construction industry, perhaps the most notorious are those shown in Table 2 (at 1980 prices).

Table 2

	Estimate (£ million)	Cost (£ million)	Difference (%)
Sydney Opera House	2.5	87	3380
Thames Barrier, London	23	400	1639
Barbican Arts Centre, London	17	80	371

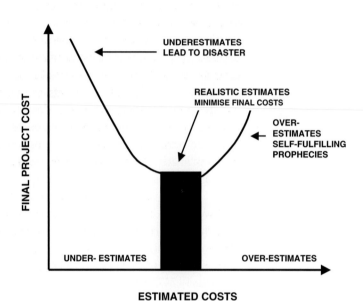

6 Freiman curve. *Source: based on Daschbach and Agpar (1988)*

Fee-bidding circle

Unlike contractors who are usually given fairly accurate drawings or bills of quantities upon which to base their calculations, the architect is at the beginning of the process. The first indication of a possibility of a job is when a prospective client indicates that he or she would like to discuss a brief for a proposed project. From this relatively scant piece of information, the architect is requested either to make a firm bid for fees or at least to give an indication of possible fee charges.

The generator of the Fee Bidding Circle (page 43) is the client's brief, which has to be clear and unambiguous. The brief is perhaps the most vital element in the entire building process, as well as the key to the fee bid. Briefs may range from the simplistic statement of 'a five-bedroomed house' etc. to the sophisticated requirements of an expert client. The RIBA (1995b) *Strategic Study* identifies the expert client as a problem for practising architects: 'Understanding the informed client who's learning fast is the biggest problem for architects.' The architect has a duty of care and will be heavily involved with the naïve client and less involved in brief preparation with the expert client. This initiating work should be paid for and clearly, in most cases, it is more than described in SFA/92: 'Obtain the Client's Requirements, Budget and Timetable.'

Green (1994) argued a case for SMART value management at the brief stage of a project based on the learning paradigm of soft systems' thinking. This is echoed by Ellegant (1992) (who uses the term 'value engineering') and suggests that

Value engineering is a formidable management tool from project inception (brief process), through design. It helps clients to articulate their requirements, creates total project understanding for the entire project team, and ensures cost effective decisions are made in harmony with the client's needs and desires.

It can be seen that the 'Obtaining of client's requirements' is both sensitive and specialized. Sensitive in that it is fundamental to the entire project and mistakes made at this stage will have disastrous effects later on. Specialized in its application. In the USA, a specialist discipline of 'programmer' has been created that exclusively prepares briefs for clients and their designers. This separate role of 'programmer' or 'brief creator' is not identified as such in the UK, and the function may be undertaken by architects, project managers, quantity surveyors or any construction consultant. Indeed, this vital role at the initiating stage of the construction process is not exploited separately within the UK construction industry. Higgins and Jessop (1965) coined the term 'sponsor' as the member of the team first approached by the client. He continued,

> The traditional first contact and sponsor of the building team is the architect. This, however, would not seem to be universal practice, particularly with sophisticated clients. We have met cases where quantity surveyors and builders have been put in the sponsor role. Other, more naïve clients, who knew only the traditional custom, and those more interested in design or function, tend to approach an architect.

For the sake of regularity and to emphasize the importance of the briefing process, the Higgins and Jessop (1965) report is hereby quoted at length, as follows:

> To ensure the ideal result from this phase of the process . . . the range of resources and techniques of communication . . . needs to be comprehensive. If the study of a client's needs – financial, aesthetic, functional and social – is to be complete, the sponsor will have to know the needs of the client very intimately, whether an individual or an organisation. He will also need to undertake a similar . . . study of relevant building resources to ensure that the best possible solutions . . . are found. The sponsor, no matter what his particular expertise, will obviously need assistance if this dual task is to be performed adequately. Even the architect, the man whom one would expect to be best qualified to undertake it, is unlikely to command sufficient knowledge, particularly in the fields of technology and costing, to be able to do it all himself. We suspect that this . . . important phase of the building process is . . . not done adequately because the original sponsor has not realised . . . the need for the application of a wider knowledge than he himself can easily command. . . .
>
> For a client who is not sophisticated in the sense in which we are using that term, it is not easy to define and communicate his needs. This is particularly true when the client is a corporate public body. The reaction of the architect, the

man usually responsible for working with the client on this job, tends to be one of frustration and impatience, largely, we suspect, from a sense of inability to help. There is often very real and unavoidable confusion for a naïve client in exploring and reconciling conflicting internal needs. There are techniques for assisting this type of process in the social sciences (problem identification, conflict resolution etc.) as well as within the industry (Stone, 1962), which we would suggest, should be better known and employed . . . Given greater understanding and tolerance by the architect of the client's confusion, and some tools for helping him, the task of preparing a brief might be done more expeditiously and more effectively. We know of one case where these conditions applied, leading to a very satisfactory outcome.

(*The Guardian* 1962).

A further description of the client was made in Jepson and Nicholson (1972):

A client may be:

1. a speculator, investing in building for profit;
2. a public body, investing in building on behalf of, or for the benefit of the community;
3. an occupier with a family, or a commercial activity or an industrial process to house; or
4. a person or body seeking a monument

The industry may offer:

1. a building on its site
2. a building for assembly on a site provided by the client
3. an assembly service for a building designed on commission to the client; or
4. one of a series of contributory services brought together and co-ordinated on behalf of the client to erect a building to a design commissioned by him.

The RIBA (1995b) *Strategic Study* referred to the encouragement of the use of feasibility studies. 'With procurement guided by options, appraisals and greater risks leading to greater caution, your profession really ought to get over how valuable a £15,000 to £30,000 feasibility study is to clients.'

The importance of the client is emphasized in Latham (1994), who asserted that 'Implementation begins with clients', and further that 'Government should commit itself to being a best practice client.' The report went on to describe the role of the client as the patron and promoter of good design (Hillman 1992). These traditional roles of the client are well established and understood. What is not so well known is that it is the client's responsibility to prepare his own brief. Whether the client be naïve or sophisticated (to use Higgins and Jessop's 1965 terminology), this brief is then 'discussed' with the architect (SFA/92). If the architect is required by the client to prepare feasibility studies or analyse and assist in constructing a brief, this is beyond the architect's job specification (RIBA 1973). All work at this stage will probably be priced on 'quantum meruit' (i.e. time and materials) before any fee bid can be prepared.

Once the client's brief has been established, the process within the Fee Bidding Circle (Figure 7) can be started. The first operation will be to prepare an outline specification and space requirement schedule. This will probably be accompanied by a few tentative layouts and feasibility design studies.

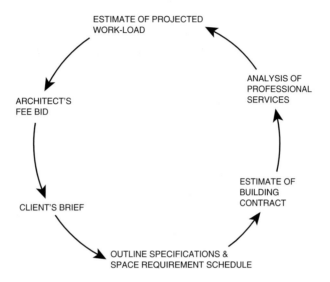

7 Fee-bidding circle: the fundamental structure of the process is circular, with all the elements being interdependent

Not only will the client need to have an indication of the costs of the proposed building, but also to assess the magnitude of the design work, the architect will need these figures. This work has been the subject of a PhD thesis by Ogunlana (1989), who studied this operation in some detail. In his conclusions, Ogunlana stated that in reference to resource-based estimating at the design phase:

> Research has progressed from elemental cost analyses through regression models to construction cost simulations and resource-based estimating. Only elemental cost analyses have been widely accepted in the industry because of its relative simplicity . . . because they can be validated using data generated in-house.

Ogunlana frequently makes reference to comparisons between the work of a design estimator and a contractor's estimator and he tries to judge their relative accuracies. The problem he does not appear to have explored is the presentation of the base material. On the one hand, the contractor's estimator is usually presented with a detailed bill of quantities prepared by a quantity surveyor in a method agreed throughout the construction industry, the Standard Method of Measurement (SMM), whereas the architect/designer's estimator at that time has only a client's brief with all its shortcomings and inaccuracies. Therefore, at this stage the architect can only hazard a guess (with the help of his quantity surveyor) about the ultimate price of the lowest or any tender which will later be offered by the contractors.

One element of CE/95 that is an obvious improvement on the earlier *Conditions of Engagement* is the detailed listing of professional services that an architect may undertake. This is a 'tick list' of possible jobs in all categories of exploration, design and supervision and can be used as a definition and analysis of an architect's professional services. It is only after the completion of these four phases (Figure 7) in the process that architects can consider producing an estimate of the resources that they will expect to be using for the proposed scheme. There is no standard procedure for this analysis, but the objective will be to divide the work down to a series of small, discrete operations and then to estimate the cost of resourcing each activity.

Estimating architects' fees

The period when the architects' (RIBA) recommended scale of fees were withdrawn left a vacuum. The author decided to investigate this area and relate the fee-bidding process of architects to the well-established methods employed by builders. The objectives of the study were:

- to introduce different methods of preparing an estimate for architectural services;
- to introduce the concepts of analytical estimating;
- to clarify the distinction between estimating and tendering; and
- to indicate market forces and competition.

The methodology was as follows:

- An examination of past records or discussions with mature and experienced architects.
- To use the traditional scales (graphs) as a basis for comparison.
- To calculate the output costs for professional charges.
- To prepare drawings' schedules as a measure of workload.
- To estimate the time allocations for elemental design/coordination/management costs.
- To prepare material suitable for tender documents for submission to a client.

The models used were benchmarking, fee scale and analytical estimating, so that each result could be compared to establish a reliable overall system to recommend to the architectural profession.

Of the twenty-four architectural practices that assisted with this work, fifteen prepared what they considered would be a reasonable schedule of drawings for the job. The estimated number of drawings ranged from thirty-two to 200 and this was the first indicator that the results of the author's enquiries amounted to what could only be described as 'wild guesses'. In fact, when questioned, the respondents all assured the writer that their submissions were genuine attempts at the truth and all were given due consideration of the tender results. Even if one disregards the highest and lowest figures, the numbers of drawings ranged from ninety-six to 189 – a difference of almost 100%. No doubt, the estimation of the number of drawings as a basis for using an analytical approach in estimating the architect's design process is valid, but it does explain the complexity of the problem and the risks involved (Norris 1992). *Faster Building for Industry* (NEDC 1983) also found a range in the numbers of drawings for similar job types – from twenty to thirty to between eighty and 100.

To ascertain the most probable and reliable fee bid, the Delphi Method of prediction was applied. It is based upon the individual opinions given by professionals (in this case designers). A calculation of the 'expected values of the individual opinions' (mathematical expectations) that are defined as the 'group opinion' was made. This actually represents a kind of average that takes into account the probability distribution (the numbers repeating) of a range of results. It provides a realistic picture of the situation in terms of identifying the most probable range of the result.

The group opinions (Ex) were calculated by using the following equation:

$$Ex = \sum xi*p(xi),$$

where xi is a random variable (in the case representing a range of individual opinions) and p(xi) is the probability distribution of the individual opinions.

Also, Ag – the difference between the group opinion (Ex) and the assumed values of the individual opinions – and the Ae – the difference between the individual opinions and the assumed exact values – can be easily calculated using the following equations:

$$Ag = wi - Ex,$$

where wi is the possible exact values (range) and

$$Ae = \sum wi - xi *p(xi).$$

The most probable expected result will fall within the range where Ag and Ae have their minimums.

As the Delphi Method of predicting is an iterative method, the whole procedure of calculating (Ex, Ag, Ae and the standard deviations in each cycle) should be repeated several times using new input (individual opinions) obtained from the same professionals (Popovic and Nicholson 1993). This has not been done in this case because of a lack of information. Nevertheless, it is obvious that the method can be applied successfully to the architectural profession and could assist clients in their task of selecting the most realistic tender rather than falling into the trap of only considering the lowest tender figure.

Discussion of the results

Scale method

Since the fee bid is based on the estimated value of the designed building, it is necessary to formulate an accurate estimate of building costs. This may not be an easy assignment, because during the evolution of the design, the building shape and size may change to some degree. Figure 8 shows the range of the fee bids obtained by this approach. It is obvious that their variances are due to the differences in the estimated building area (although it is the same design brief) and price per square metre.

DESIGN TIME

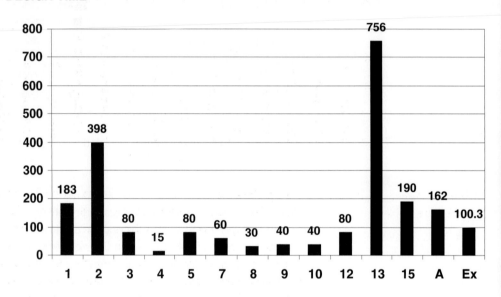

8 Different architects' assessments of design times for the same building

It can also be seen that Ex represents the most probable range of results better than the simple average. However, if the input (the estimated area of the building) was more accurate, then it would have been obvious that this approach provides no competition among the architects because of the fixed values of their fee bids. Unfortunately, the available data do not show this. It is probably due to this lack of ability to estimate building values that many architects continue to bid on a percentage basis related to the estimated final cost of the building.

Analytical method

The fee bid obtained by the analytical approach also varies considerably (Figure 9). The reason for this kind of output is because the variables upon which it depends also differ widely. For example, the maximum value of the annual cost is seven times greater than the minimum. In addition, the size of the organization in terms of technical employees as well as the price per man-day indicate considerable variations.

An attempt has been made to find out how the size of an organization affects the price per man-day. Perhaps the most significant finding is that within this

SCALE METHOD
Ex10³ BID

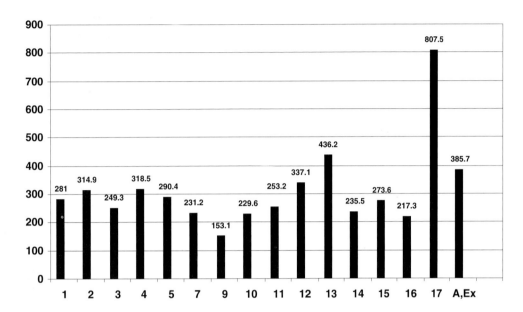

9 Fee bids by the scale method for the same building

sample, the larger organizations cost more per productive person than do the smaller firms – there does not appear to be economy of scale.

The average price per man-day is calculated in different ways and the most expected value, Ex, is variable (Figure 10). Because of the nature of the design process (as discussed above), it was likely that there would be a large variation in the data concerning the number of necessary drawings as well as in the total time required to finish the job. Schedules of drawings have been used for a long time to estimate the man-hours needed for the detail design and production drawing stages. However, production drawings and specifications represent only the output of design work; more than half of a design process is spent gathering information, developing preliminary designs and verifying the consistency of work (at all stages). In scheduling the entire process, this 'silent majority' of the workload must be taken into account (Spekkink 1993).

The reason for the wide variation in individual opinions of the sample practices is because there is no developed methodology that defines how to estimate the architect's design work. If such an accurate methodology is to be developed, then the following bias must be overcome (Coles 1992):

- That it is impossible to estimate and plan the design work.
- That architects are obstructed by factors beyond their control.
- That methods that attempt to put architects' design work into a mould will inhibit their creativity.
- The fear that data collection and analytical analysis will consume more time and energy than it is worth.

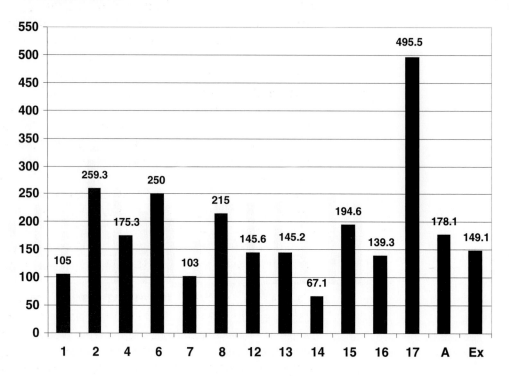

£x10³
ANNUAL COSTS

10 Annual man-day costs estimated by 17 architectural practices

The strength of the analytical approach is that it breaks down the total operation into small parts, each of which is easier to comprehend than the totality of the job. Here, the work has been broken down into the unit of a drawing and the number of drawings has been used as a basis for calculation. This at least provides a common basis by which to test the results; yet the survey showed that there was no consensus between architectural practices about the numbers of drawings that may be required for each job – this is an area for further research.

Although it has failings in the architectural context, the analytical method, if considered as an approach, appears to be the best and as such should be developed and implemented. In addition, when such a method is developed, a database of fee bids should be established. These 'benchmark' fees obtained in such a way will gain in their reliability and credibility. The percentage scale method will fade into non-use or act as a guide only to check against calculated bids.

Fees and finances

Even a brief investigation will prove that the traditional working method of the architect and the standard Architects' Appointment offer clearly defined rules for fees. The percentage fees are based on construction costs, i.e. from the point of view of the client it is not fixed and can escalate if there are variations (some of which may arise from design). The fee varies with the extent of services, the complexity of the work type and the value of the finished product. Partial fees are charged for partial services. The percentage fees charged in 1990 are, in 99% of cases in a recent survey, all less than those recommended by the RIBA (Naamani 1990). They ranged from 9.80% (the highest) to 5.75% for an £800,000 industrial building. Other methods are lump sums for prescribed areas of work, and day work at agreed rates of pay, by the hour, day or week.

The architectural profession is now faced with commercial decisions, keen competition and a new position in the market place. Saint (1983) noted that fear of the open market place would lead to protectionism by architects rather than to a commercial approach. 'Perhaps the need to promote change was not felt strongly enough at the RIBA, or amongst its members in the past' (Emmitt and Neary 1995).

Fee competition among the industry's professional practices has now been established. A survey of 327 professional services firms across all disciplines undertaken by *New Builder* (McLellan 1994) indicated that more than one-third of firms now gain more than 70% of their workload on a competitive fee basis. Since 1991, the number gaining 70% of commissions through this route has risen from 14 to 39%. As well as the unprecedented swing towards competitive bidding, the number of firms securing the bulk of their commissions on a negotiated basis has changed. Only 29% of the sample now negotiate more than 70% of their workload as opposed to 55% in 1991.

The CIC Practice Committee is in the process of completing a second major guide to the management of fee tendering by clients. This guide advises clients to give equal or greater weight to quality factors such as innovative design and life-cycle costs when considering fee bids. Still critical of its own system of payment and reward, the RIBA (1995b) *Strategic Study* comments: 'Any system which rewards someone for spending more money is barmy. If during the course of design a building becomes more complex, the fee should go down, not up.' The *Study* further suggested that architects should 'expect incentive schemes to proliferate in the future'.

State of the art

To discover the amount of fee-tendering activity by UK architects, a survey was undertaken in 1995 (Table 3). Although some respondents indicated they did not answer questionnaires relating to commercial issues, a significant number of architects did reply. An overall positive response rate of 42% was achieved from a simple mailing, and this would approximate to the number of architectural practices in the UK.

Table 3

Size of firm (number of architects)	Replies (%)
0	5
1–5	57
6–10	12
11–20	12
21–50	14
51+	0

The survey held no surprises about the responsibilities for undertaking the estimating/tendering function. In 89% of the respondent firms, the estimator of fees was the senior partner/director, while only 11% of firms allowed their project architects to take this responsibility. It was interesting that two firms, in the 1–5 size, had specialist estimator/surveyors; one an RICS (QS Division), the other was qualified as MSc RIBA – both estimators would therefore appear to have specialist knowledge and skills in estimating. The implication could be extended to suggest that 97% of the total survey had no prior education in the subject, and only 3% had possibly received any formal education in estimating.

The questionnaire asked the practices the number of estimates they prepared each week, or how many they prepared, on average, during a typical month. Almost half (42%) of the firms said that they submitted one tender a week, with a further one-quarter (26%) producing two tenders a week. Of the remainder, 14% prepared four tenders a week, while 18% performed one every 2–3 weeks. This would indicate a very high incidence of estimating function within the sample as described in this survey. Further research at regular intervals would be an indicator of estimating activity, and changes could be identified.

If 83% of all architectural practices are submitting between one and four tenders a week, it would be interesting to know how much time each week was devoted to the activity and whether it took up a significant part of the estimator's working week.

The average for this survey is just over one estimate a week. It is possible that this high rate of activity would militate against the adoption of more detailed techniques than a glance at an 'indicative' fee scale chart owing to time commitments and other responsibilities. Two-thirds of the respondents said that they used fee scales as a basis for their estimates.

The survey asked the respondents to give the values of their last three bids; one-third of the replies indicated that the bids were less than £10,000. A further 41% were between £10,000 and £50,000, with the remainder being over £50,000. If one calculates the mid-point in each range of figures and divides that by the total responses ($n = 123$), the average bid within the survey was £60,146. Extrapolating this further, £60,000 at a frequency rate of one each week (working a 40-week year), would mean an average yearly turnover (assuming half of the bids were successful) of £120,000, or if only one in five bids were successful, a £48,000 turnover.

Only accurate figures would allow this discussion to continue, but one might generalize and suggest that as the majority of architectural practices employ about ten technical staff, that their income would need to be 10 × £50,000 = £500,000 – well within the 'guestimate' range of incomes.

Again, the distribution of fee bids will probably change over time and this would prove a useful area for further research. The survey (1995) indicated that practices employing 0–5 technical staff priced mainly jobs up to £10,000, with a spread up to £250,000. In the survey, the practices employing 6–10 technical staff did not bid (in their last three bids) under £10,000, but one-third of their fee bids were more than £250,000. The group of practices that employed 11–20 technical staff did not have any results over £250,000. Instead, they devoted their energies (over one-quarter) to bids of less than £10,000. Sixty per cent of the fee-bidding output of this 11–20 person group was for bids between £10,000 and £50,000.

Predictably, the group of largest practices (employing 21–50 technical staff) did not quote for fees below £10,000. Fifty per cent of their output was in fee bids between £10,000 and £50,000, with the remainder of their bids being more than £100,000, including 21% over £250,000. Again, this group indicated that, on average, one bid was submitted a week. With £100,000 and £250,000, the workload in estimating fee bids must take up a considerable amount of management time if it is done thoroughly and in some detail.

Estimating method

Respondents to the fee-bidding survey were asked to state which methods of analysis or support they used in the preparation of bids, ranging from a calculation of man-weeks to pure guesswork (29% admitted to a degree of guesswork). Two-thirds of respondents said they used the fee scales as a basis for tenders, and 76% replied that previous fee bids were used as benchmarks for further tendering. Two-thirds of respondents looked to their own experience for help with fee tendering.

The business environment has changed during the period of this study and estimating skills for fee bids are now required of the architectural profession. The standard scale fees were used by only 13% of respondents to the fee-bidding survey. More sophisticated analysis of fee bidding is now used within all sections of the profession, yet the education provision does not reflect the level of input required. Education, therefore, has not kept pace with practice management requirements.

The fact that all categories of firms indicated a low dependence on fee scales would imply that architectural practices are now looking to other, more sophisticated methods of fee calculation. All of the groups of practices replied that they made calculations as estimates of time (in man-weeks) and all groups (except the smallest one) indicated that they used drawings' registers as a measurement of their workload.

Part II Worked examples

A The probable building cost

B Calculating the fees – *ad valorem*

C Analytical estimating of fees

D Analysis and conclusions

A The probable building cost

Introduction

It is probably true to say that all clients of construction operations need to have a good idea of the costs involved in a project. According to Hyams (2001), 'Clients are likely to ask about cost from the first day.' Few people or organizations are in a position to act as patron and offer an open chequebook for the work. Nowadays, finance will enter the conversation at an early stage, and promises have to be met.

The architect, however, is in a very difficult position when asked for a fixed (guaranteed) fee. The architect is being asked to determine the price of undertaking the design work of a building not in existence. The building will have unique design features and it will be constructed on a new site, by unknown (at this stage) builders, in uncertain weather conditions, by a fragmented supply industry. Add to that the uncertainties that may frustrate or interrupt the process by a client, even an experienced client, and the task appears to be placing a huge risk on all concerned.

To some extent, when presented with a set of drawings and a bill of quantities, the builders do have an advantage over the designer. Builders have been estimating prices for their work for over two centuries. Databases have been built up and books printed with detailed pricing information, so that the pricing of building operations can be reasonably well estimated. However, no such information is available to the architect, particularly the inexperienced architect who can offer only a wild guess and hope that the work will bring in a living wage.

For too long, architects have relied on cheap labour from students who are asked to work extra hours when a job is running into debt. Moreover, architecture is the only profession that *expects* staff to work considerable overtime without adequate remuneration. It has been said in Hong Kong, for example, that overtime payment starts at 22:00 hours! It is due entirely to the inaccuracies in estimating fees that the architectural profession relies to a large extent on the enthusiasm and vocational loyalties of its staff to see a job through. It must be remembered that architecture is a business and firms need to show a profit to survive.

Methodology

Estimating the building cost

The worked example of fee bidding starts from the point where an initial investigation has been undertaken and feasibility studies discussed and agreed with the clients. This work may have been undertaken either by another firm or by yourselves, probably on a charge-by-the-day basis. Therefore, certain basic facts are given in the worked example for building details shown on page 57.

Detailed drawings of the existing building (a former technical college annex) are available.

In this case, there has been a feasibility study previously undertaken by the client. This will reduce some of the uncertainties that otherwise may be added features of a designer's risks, but if no feasibility study has previously been commissioned, then it will form an additional element of the work for the architect.

Location: South West of England
Client: university medical school
Building: part conversion of an existing building, part two-storey
Site: within a city campus, on a very tight site; subsoil
Planning: outline planning permission has been granted
Conditions: existing drainage and services have been located
                   new build; high security

Gross area (m²)

New buildings	3,295
Existing teaching block	1,317
Existing out-buildings	160
Total	4,772

Contract

Design services:	CE'99
Building contract:	JCT'98
Including:	
Furniture:	£452,983
Incinerator:	£195,010
Contingencies:	£138,645

Fee bid required

Full design and supervision £10,000 to be included for archaeological exploration works
Excluding:
    Quantity surveyor
    Structural engineer
    M&E engineer
    Landscape architect

Programme

Archaeological exploration	2	months
Full design works	14	months
Builders' tender period	1	month
Tender decision	1	month
Construction work	19	months
Loose furniture and fittings	1	month
Total	36	months (excluding archaeological exploration)

Cost of the building works

At this stage it is necessary to estimate, as accurately as possible, the probable cost of the building works, i.e. construction costs without professional and other fees. This figure will enable the client to prepare a budget for expenditure and, at the same time, it will become a constraint for the designer.

There are four methods of pricing construction (Figure 11):

* Precedence studies: using examples of previous similar types of buildings to produce a preliminary estimate of the cost of the building contract.
* Price books and published texts such as *Spon's Architects' & Builders' Price Book* (2000) (Spain 2000). Calculations are made either from a detailed analysis of the separate components of the proposed building, or they are based on floor and paved areas, etc.
* Benchmark pricing from practising quantity surveyors, based on experience of previous costs.
* Building Cost Information Service (BCIS): quarterly review figures from the BICS provide a mean, mode and range cost per square metre (m^2) for a wide variety of CI/SfB-classified building types.

Precedent studies (Method 1)

Precedent studies: analysis

Table 4

Precedent study building	Building type	Regional factor (UK mean 1.0)	Total cost (£ millions)	Area (m^2)	Cost (£/m^2)
Institute for Biomedical Science, Glasgow	Education, Class 5 (University laboratories)	Glasgow (1.01)	8.80	8,970	990
Synthetic Chemistry Labs, Bristol	Education, Class 5 (University laboratories)	Bristol (0.97)	11.65	7,287	1,599
International Building, Royal Holloway College, Surrey	Education, Class 4 (University complexes)	Surrey (1.05)	2.65	3,460	765

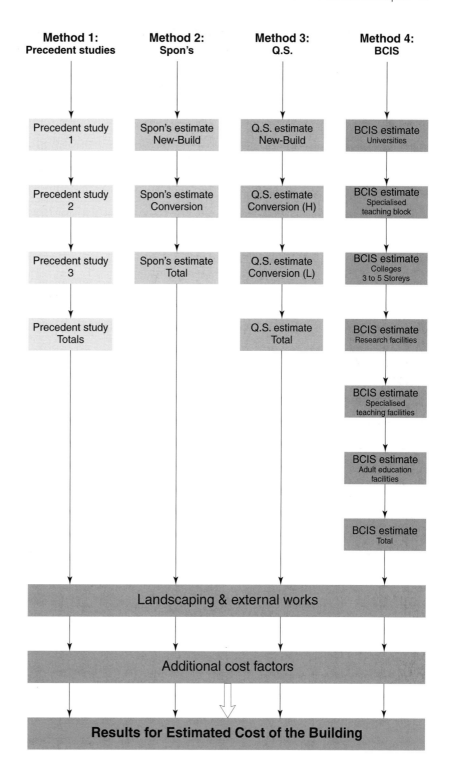

Method 1:
Precedent studies

Method 2:
Spon's

Method 3:
Q.S.

Method 4:
BCIS

Precedent study
1

Precedent study
2

Precedent study
3

Precedent study
Totals

Spon's estimate
New-Build

Spon's estimate
Conversion

Spon's estimate
Total

Q.S. estimate
New-Build

Q.S. estimate
Conversion (H)

Q.S. estimate
Conversion (L)

Q.S. estimate
Total

BCIS estimate
Universities

BCIS estimate
Specialised
teaching block

BCIS estimate
Colleges
3 to 5 Storeys

BCIS estimate
Research facilities

BCIS estimate
Specialised
teaching facilities

BCIS estimate
Adult education
facilities

BCIS estimate
Total

Landscaping & external works

Additional cost factors

Results for Estimated Cost of the Building

11 Methodology diagram

Precedent studies: total

Table 5

Precedent study building	Cost (£/m²)	Regional factor (UK mean 1.0)	Area of project building (m²)	Total
Institute for Biomedical Science, Glasgow	990	1.01	7,205	(990 × 7,205 × 1.04) = 6,918,961
Synthetic Chemistry Labs, Bristol	1,599	0.97	7,205	(1,599 × 7,205) = 11,520,795
International Building, Royal Holloway College, Surrey	765	1.05	7,205	(765 × 7,205 × 1.08) = 5,952,771
Average for precedent studies (inclusive of all preliminaries, external works and contingencies)				£8,130,842 (£1,128.50/m²)

Preliminary estimate from Spon's price book (Method 2)

Prices do not allow for external works, furniture, loose or special equipment and are exclusive of fees for professional services.

Spon's estimate: new build

Table 6

Building type (new build) (as classified under CI/SfB 7 Educational, Scientific, Information Facilities)	Cost (£/m²) (excluding VAT)	Average cost (£/m²) (excluding VAT)
Polytechnics: scientific laboratories	845–1,060	952.50
Universities: science buildings	870–1,125	997.50
Laboratories and offices, low-level servicing	785–985	885
Average		945

Therefore, the preliminary cost for the new-build component of a building is:

$$5,195 \times 945 = 4,909,275$$

Spon's estimate: conversion

Table 7

Building type (conversion)	Cost (£/m²) (excluding VAT)	Average cost (£/m²) (excluding VAT)
Office refurbishment	515–700	607.50
Museums, conversion to a regional standard	670–1,020	845
Estimated average for a veterinary school	800	800
Average		800

Therefore, the preliminary cost for conversion component of a building is:

$$2,010 \times 800 = £1,608,000$$

Spon's estimate: total

Preliminary cost for the new-build component of a building = £4,909,275
Preliminary cost for the conversion component of a building = £1,608,000
Total estimate from Spon's preliminary cost guide (exclusive of external works, professional fees and contingency sums) = **£6,517,275**.

Preliminary estimate from a chartered surveyor (Method 3)

Quantity surveyor estimate: new build

Table 8

Building element	Baseline estimate (£/m²)	Total area (m²)	Estimate (£)
Building costs	900	5,195	4,675,500
Fittings	65	5,195	337,675
Drainage	–	–	35,000
Incoming costs	–	–	20,000
Total			**5,068,175**

Quantity surveyor estimate: conversion (with high knowledge of the existing structure)

Table 9

Building element	Baseline estimate (£/m²)	Total area (m²)	Estimate (£)
Building costs	450	2,010	904,500
Fittings	65	2,010	130,650
Drainage	–	–	included
Incoming costs	–	–	included
Total			**1,035,150**

Quantity surveyor estimate: conversion (with low knowledge of the existing structure)

Table 10

Building element	Baseline estimate (£/m²)	Total area (m²)	Estimate (£)
Building costs	600	2,010	1,206,000
Fittings	65	2,010	130,650
Drainage	–	–	included
Incoming costs	–	–	included
Total (conservative estimate)			**1,336,650**

Quantity surveyor estimate: total

Table 11

Building element	Estimate (£)
New build	5,068,175
Conversion (conservative estimate)	1,336,650
Total	6,404,825

The total is inclusive of drainage and incoming services, preliminaries, new build and conversion. It is exclusive of all other external works, a contingency sum, statutory fees, and architects' and consultants' fees.

In the quantity surveyor calculation, one of the unknowns and consequent high risks is the amount of survey work and structural alterations that may be needed in the conversion of the existing building. Therefore, in this case, it was decided to take the higher of the two figures for conversion costs.

Other situations may suggest either an average of the two possibilities or, if the job appears to be quite straightforward, then the lower figure may be used.

Building Cost Information Service (BCIS) quarterly review figures (Method 4)

Introduction

The BCIS was set up by the Royal Institution of Chartered Surveyors to facilitate the exchange of detailed cost information between chartered quantity surveyors so that, by pooling their information, they could have the best available databank when providing advice to their clients.

The BCIS provides detailed mean, mode and range costs ($£/m^2$) for a wide variety of CI/SfB-classified building types. The figures quoted in the BCIS quarterly reviews are based upon tender price analysis of approximately 5,000 buildings. The figures are for contract sums including preliminary sums, but excluding external works and contingencies sums.

CI/SfB building types

Results from the BCIS reviews are collated for the following building types:

Table 12

CI/SfB no. (C)	Building type	New build (N) or conversion
721	CI/SfB 7 Educational, Scientific, Information Facilities: Universities	N
721.2	CI/SfB 7 Educational, Scientific, Information Facilities: University – Specialized Teaching Blocks	N
722	CI/SfB 7 Educational, Scientific, Information Facilities: Colleges – 3 to 5 Storeys	N
731.1	CI/SfB 7 Educational, Scientific, Information Facilities: Research Facilities	N
713.1	Rehabilitation/Conversion: Specialized Teaching Blocks	C
727	Rehabilitation/Conversion: Adult Education Facilities	C

Variables

Two variables are required to adjust the figures for a specified project:

- Tender price index
- Regional factors.

Tender price index

The tender price index measures the trend of contractors' pricing levels in accepted tenders for new work. The predicted tender price index for the fourth quarter of 2000 is 162 (*Architects Journal* 1998, 9 July, 45). As BCIS journals are only available locally up to the fourth quarter of 1996, the tender price index is included in the conversion calculation and thus still affords a good indication of current building costs.

12 UK regional factors.
Source: Mason, unpublished dissertation

Regional factors

The variable for regional factor allows for the effect of location on building cost.

Calculations: example

The approximate estimate of a building cost is:

> [mean (£/m^2) × location factor] gross internal floor area (m^2) forecast tender price/estimate tender price

BCIS estimate: 721 Universities

Table 13

Date	Tender price Bench project	Regional adjustment Specific project	Mean cost (£/m^2) Bench project	Project floor area (m^2) Specific project	Total (£) Bench project	Specific project		
Latest figures available	132	162	1	0.97	751	728.47	3,295	2,328,299
	133	162	1	0.97	759	736.23	3,295	2,353,102
	131	162	1	0.97	753	730.41	3,295	2,334,500
	126	162	1	0.97	721	699.37	3,295	2,235,291
	126	162	1	0.97	721	699.37	3,295	2,235,291
	122	162	1	0.97	689	668.33	3,295	2,136,083
	116	162	1	0.97	655	635.35	3,295	2,030,674
	114	162	1	0.97	644	624.68	3,295	1,996,571
							Average total	2,206,226
							Average (£/m^2)	669.57

By way of example, note that the numbers may rise or fall.

BCIS estimate: 721.2 University – Specialized Teaching Blocks

Table 14

Date	Tender price Bench project	Regional adjustment Specific project	Mean cost (£/m^2) Bench project	Project floor area (m^2) Specific project	Total (£) Bench project	Specific project		
Latest figures available	132	162	1	0.97	799	775.03	3,295	2,477,112
	133	162	1	0.97	806	781.82	3,295	2,498,814
	131	162	1	0.97	813	788.61	3,295	2,520,516
	126	162	1	0.97	749	726.53	3,295	2,322,099
	126	162	1	0.97	751	728.47	3,295	2,348,299
	122	162	1	0.97	723	701.31	3,295	2,241,492
	116	162	1	0.97	696	675.12	3,295	2,157,785
	114	162	1	0.97	682	661.54	3,295	2,114,381
							Average total	2,332,562
							Average (£/m^2)	707.91

BCIS estimate: 722 Colleges – 3 to 5 Storeys

Table 15

Date	Tender price Bench project	Regional adjustment Specific project	Mean cost (£/m²) Bench project	Project floor area (m²) Specific project	Total (£) Bench project	Specific project		
Latest figures available	132	162	1	0.97	659	639.23	3,295	2,043,075
	133	162	1	0.97	666	646.02	3,295	2,064,777
	131	162	1	0.97	656	636.32	3,295	2,033,774
	126	162	1	0.97	632	613.04	3,295	1,959,368
	126	162	1	0.97	630	611.1	3,295	1,953,167
	122	162	1	0.97	613	594.61	3,295	1,900,463
	116	162	1	0.97	581	563.57	3,295	1,801,252
	114	162	1	0.97	571	553.87	3,295	1,770,252
						Average total		1,940,765
						Average (£/m²)		589

BCIS estimate: 731.1 Research Facilities

Table 16

Date	Tender price Bench project	Regional adjustment Specific project	Mean cost (£/m²) Bench project	Project floor area (m²) Specific project	Total (£) Bench project	Specific project		
Latest figures available	132	162	1	0.97	830	805.1	3,295	2,573,220
	133	162	1	0.97	836	810.95	3,295	2,591,918
	131	162	1	0.97	825	800.25	3,295	2,557,719
	126	162	1	0.97	791	767.27	3,295	2,452,310
	126	162	1	0.97	791	767.27	3,295	2,452,310
	122	162	1	0.97	759	736.23	3,295	2,353,102
	116	162	1	0.97	736	713.92	3,295	2,281,795
	114	162	1	0.97	721	699.37	3,295	2,235,291
						Average total		2,437,221
						Average (£/m²)		739,67

BCIS estimate: 713.1 Specialized Teaching Blocks

Table 17

Date	Tender price Bench project	Regional adjustment Specific project	Mean cost (£/m²) Bench project	Project floor area (m²) Specific project	Total (£) Bench project	Specific project		
	132	162	1	0.97	354	343.38	1,477	491,957
	133	162	1	0.97	353	342.41	1,477	490,567
	131	162	1	0.97	336	325.92	1,477	505,625
	126	162	1	0.97	325	315.25	1,477	451,656
	126	162	1	0.97	323	313.31	1,477	448,876
	122	162	1	0.97	311	301.67	1,477	432,200
	116	162	1	0.97	293	284.21	1,477	355,608
	114	162	1	0.97	293	284.21	1,477	407,185

(Latest figures available)

Average total 447,959
Average (£/m²) 303.29

BCIS estimate: 727 Adult Education Facilities

Table 18

Date	Tender price Bench project	Regional adjustment Specific project	Mean cost (£/m²) Bench project	Project floor area (m²) Specific project	Total (£) Bench project	Specific project		
	132	162	1	0.97	377	365.69	1,477	523,920
	133	162	1	0.97	378	366.66	1,477	525,310
	131	162	1	0.97	370	358.9	1,477	514,192
	126	162	1	0.97	356	345.32	1,477	494,737
	126	162	1	0.97	356	345.32	1,477	494,737
	122	162	1	0.97	343	332.71	1,477	476,670
	116	162	1	0.97	325	315.25	1,477	451,656

(Latest figures available)

Average total 495,889
Average (£/m²) 335.70

BCIS results: new build

Table 19

Cl/SfB no.	Building type	Building area (m²)	Average cost (£)	Average total cost (£/m²)
721	Cl/SfB 7 Educational, Scientific, Information Facilities: Universities	5,195	2,206,226	670
721.2	Cl/SfB 7 Educational, Scientific, Information Facilities: University – Specialized Teaching Blocks	5,195	2,332,562	708
722	Cl/SfB 7 Educational, Scientific, Information Facilities: Colleges – 3 to 5 Storeys	5,195	1,940,765	589
731.1	Cl/SfB 7 Educational, Scientific, Information Facilities: Research Facilities	5,195	2,437,221	740
		Totals	2,229,194	677

BCIS results: conversion

Table 20

Cl/SfB no.	Building type	Building area (m²)	Average cost (£)	Average total cost (£/m²)
713.1	Rehabilitation/Conversion: Specialized Teaching Blocks	2,010	447,959	303
727	Rehabilitation/Conversion: Adult Education Facilities	2,010	495,889	336
		Totals	471,924	319

BCIS results: total building cost

Therefore, from the BCIS data, the total cost of the new build and conversion of the building would be:

New build: £2,229,194
Conversion: £471,924
Total: £2,701,118

This figure is the total contract sum for building works including preliminaries, but excluding external works, a contingency sum, statutory fees, professional fees and value-added tax (VAT) where applicable.

Landscaping and external works (Spon's)

Cost calculation for landscaping and external works

Table 21

Item	Area (m²)	Cost (£/m²)	Total (£)
1. Site clearing (vegetation, bushes, scrub, undergrowth, etc.)	4,025	0.26	1,046.5
2. Site excavation (by machine, topsoil for preservation)	4,025	1.18	4,749.5
3. Drainage (excavating trenches, grading bottoms, refilling, etc.)	2,000	22.45	44,900
4. Roads (tarmacadam finish, two lanes, 7.30 m wide, urban, inclusive)	2,000	1,345 /m	368,493
5. Paving (concrete rectangular blocks)	400	18.12	7,280
6. Top soil (150 mm thick)	550	1.84	1,012
7. Seeding	550	0.61	335.5
8. Fencing	292 m	31.10 /m	9,081
Total			436,898

Data are from Spon (2000).

Additional cost factors affecting the total contract value

Preliminaries

The following preliminary sums are calculated for inclusion with certain methods of cost calculation. Provisional sums are to include totals for the following:

- Site administration
- Defects after completion
- Insurance of the works against fire, etc.
- Clerk of works' office
- Additional management and staff
- Contractor's accommodation
- Lighting and power for the works
- Water for the works
- Temporary telephones
- Safety, health and welfare
- Removing rubbish, etc. and cleaning
- Drying the works
- Small plant and tools
- Personnel transport
- Scaffolding
- Temporary hoardings.

The total value of preliminaries may vary between 11 and 13% of the total tender value. Spon (2000) recommends 11% addition for preliminaries to be applied to the total contract value.

Contingency sums

A contingency sum is added to the total contract value to account for any unspecified occurrences during the contract. In this example, 5% has been added, but if there are a number of possible variations a higher percentage may be included.

Value-added tax (VAT)

Owing to the charitable status of universities, the cost of this contract would be zero-rated for VAT.

Inflation

Assuming an 18-month contract duration, with 6 months' design time, an additional 2.5% will be added to account for inflationary rises. This percentage should be extrapolated from known movements in inflation whenever possible.

Estimated value of the building contract

Contract estimation methods: results' comparison

Table 22

Contract estimation method	Average cost ($£/m^2$)	Estimate total ($£$)	Additional factors	Total ($£$)
Precedent studies (Method 1)	1,128.5	5,335,382	Inclusive of: preliminaries, external works and contingencies Exclusive of: (1) Inflation (2.5%)	5,468,767
Preliminary estimate from Spon's price book (Method 2)	904.5	4,186,816	Exclusive of: (1) External works = £436,898 (2) Preliminaries (11%) = £719,900 (3) Contingency sum (5%, of 7,674,073) = £383,703 (4) Inflation (2.5%)	5,353,482
Preliminary estimate from a chartered quantity surveyor (Method 3)	889	4,231,880	Inclusive of: preliminaries, site drainage Exclusive of: (1) Remaining external works = £400,000 (2) Contingency sum (5%) = £340,241 (3) Inflation (2.5%)	4,889,788
Building Cost Information Service (BCIS) quarterly review figures (Method 4)	770	2,701,118	Inclusive of: preliminaries Exclusive of: (1) External works = £436,898 (2) Contingency sum (5%) = £299,344 (3) Inflation (2.5%)	3,358,577

Contract estimation methods: analysis

Table 23

Contract estimation method	Advantages	Disadvantages	Order of method preference
Precedent studies (Method 1)	Current, quick	General, small sample size	3
Preliminary estimate from Spon's price book (Method 2)	Quick	Preliminary results	4
Preliminary estimate from a chartered quantity surveyor (Method 3)	Experienced estimate, quick	Preliminary estimate	2
Building Cost Information Service (BCIS) quarterly review figures (Method 4)	Accurate, adjustable figures, large sample size	Complex	

For the purposes of this exercise, the BCIS figures are used to estimate the approximate value of this building contract as follows:

New build:	£2,229,194
Conversion:	£471,924
External works:	£436,898
Contingencies:	£138,645
Furniture:	£452,983
Incinerator:	£195,010
Archaeological exploration:	£10,000
Total building contract:	£3,934,654 (rounded to £4 million)

Statutory approval costs for client information

Planning fee

Under The Town and Country Planning Regulation 1997, PART II: Scale of fees, our building is classified as a Category 2 building, qualifying for £190 for each 75 m² of proposed development to a maximum of £9,500. Therefore:

Total area of proposal = 4,772/75 × 190 = £12,089.

Therefore, the maximum planning fee applies = £9,500.

Building regulations' fee

Estimated cost of total building contract:	£3,934,654	
Less contingencies:	£138,645	
Less archaeology:	£10,000	
Less inflation factor:	£81,916	(subtotal £230,561)
Total:	£3,704,093	

(The estimated cost for the building regulations' fee calculation to exclude any professional fees and VAT.)

Table 24

Building regulations' fee type	Basic (£) £1 million contract value (£)	Additional fee per £1,000 over	Total additional fee (£)	Total fee payable (£)
Plan fee	1,020	0.90	2,434	3,454
Inspection fee	3,070	2.60	7,031	10,101
		Total		26,571 (including VAT)

It is important to notify the client at an early stage of his or her financial liability for planning and building regulation fees for the project. If these figures are included in the fee bid, then this should be clearly stated.

Having taken previously the decision to use the BCIS figures for building works, the study of an appropriate fee bid can be based on the approximate figure of £4 million for the construction contract. This basic information will be used for all future calculations in this exercise.

The next reference should be the architect's plan of work, and a consideration of the extent of the architect's services. The *Architect's Plan of Work* (RIBA 2000), Part 2, is prepared for 'a consultant team operation relating to the traditional fully designed procurement route'. It provides guidance for each work stage and for the sequence of operations of the designers. Whilst this document cannot cover every eventuality, it may be used in conjunction with RIBA's architect/client 'conditions of engagement'.

B Calculating the fees –
ad valorem

Introduction

Two methods were used to study the use of traditional fee scales and produce a percentage fee for the project. First, the RIBA indicative percentage fee scales were used, and the results compiled and presented. To act as a control, Spon's indicative percentage fees index was used from *Spon's Architects' & Builders' Price Book* (2000).

Methodology

The methodology is shown in the methodology diagram (Figure 13).

RIBA indicative percentage fee scales (Method 1)

Fee scales

Fee scales are no longer recommended nor even advised, but they do provide a useful indication of the type of fees that may be charged for architect services. This exercise uses two sets of indicative fee scales: the RIBA indicative percentage fee scales and Spon's fee index.

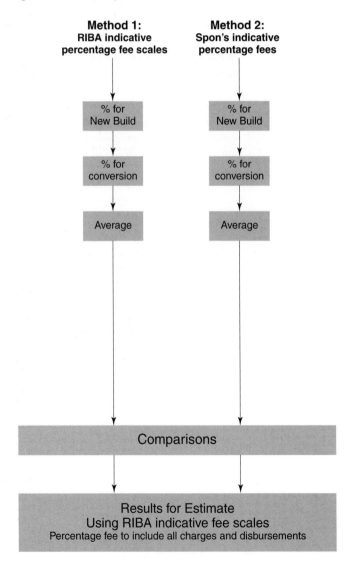

13 Methodology diagram

Classification of building type

Table 25

Type	Class 1	Class 2	Class 3	Class 4	Class 5
Industrial	• Storage sheds	• Speculative factories and warehouses • Assembly and machine workshops • Transport garages	•Purpose-built factories and warehouses		
Agriculture	• Barns and sheds	• Stables	• Animal-breeding units		
Commerical	• Speculative shops • Surface car parks	• Multistorey and underground car parks	• Supermarkets • Banks • Purpose-built shops • Office developments • Retail warehouses • Garages/showrooms	• Department stores • Shopping centres • Food-processing units • Breweries Telecommunications and computer buildings • Restaurants • Public houses	• High risk research and production building • Research and development laboratories • Radio, television and recording studios
Community		• Community halls	• Community centres • Branch libraries • Ambulance and fire stations • Bus/railway stations • Airports • Police stations • Prisons • Postal buildings • Broadcasting	• Civic centres • Churches and crematoria • Specialist libraries • Museums and art galleries • Magistrates/county courts	• Theatres • Opera houses • Concert halls • Cinemas • Crown courts
Residential		• Dormitory hotels	• Estates housing and flats • Barracks • Sheltered housing • Housing for single people • Student housing	• Parsonages/manses • Apartment blocks • Hotels • Housing for the handicapped • Housing for the frail elderly	• Houses and flats for individual clients
Education			• Primary/nursery/first schools	• Other schools including middle and secondary • University complexes	• University laboratories
Recreation			• Sports halls • Squash courts	• Swimming pools • Leisure complexes	• Leisure pools • Specialized complexes
Medical/social services			• Clinics	• Health centres • General hospitals • Nursing homes • Surgeries	• Teaching hospitals • Hospital laboratories • Dental surgeries

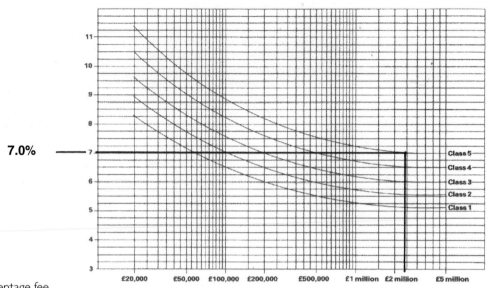

7.0%

14 Indicative percentage fee scale: new build. *Source: RIBA (1990)*

£2,229,194

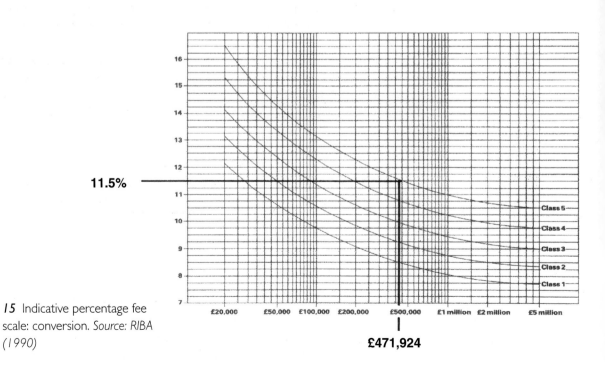

11.5%

15 Indicative percentage fee scale: conversion. *Source: RIBA (1990)*

£471,924

Indicative percentage fee scale: conversion

Summary of results

RIBA indicative percentage fee scale

Table 26

			Fee
7.0% of New build		2,229,194	156,044
11.5% of Conversion		471,924	54,271
Total building work		2,701,118	210,315
External works (e.g. 6% fees)		436,898	26,214
Contingencies			
(2.5% supervision-only fee)	138,645	786,638	19,666
Furniture (2.5%)	452,983		
Incinerator (2.5%)	195,010		
Archaeology (1% nominal fee)		19,700	197
Total building contract		**3,924,654**	
Lump sum fee			**256,392**
Expressed as an overall percentage =			
256,392/3,924,654 × 100 = **6.53%**			

The debate about the publication of fee scales, even if they are described as 'indicative', continues to rage; the RIBA argues that clients need some guidance on fee charges and that the publication of the scales indicates a national minimum. The reality is that few architects (except the signature architects) feel that they can aspire to the published scales, so they offer their clients a 'discounted' fee, i.e. one below that recommended on the scales.

However, the Office of Fair Trading (OFT) is not keen on fee scales' guidance and it completed a review in September 2001: 'One of its recommendations is that the RIBA does away with its fee scale guidance documents.' Previously, when describing fee scales as a method of fee guidance, HM Treasury (1997) wrote:

> *ad valorem* fee structures reimburse consultants in proportion (generally as a percentage) of the cost of the project. They appear to provide an incentive for consultants to design expensive projects, rather than those offering best value for money.

An indictment indeed!

Lump sum or percentage fee

Submitting a fee-bid tender as a lump sum or percentage fee could be stipulated in the invitation to tender documents received from the client. Both lump sum and percentage fees have advantages and disadvantages for the architect. In simplistic terms, the risk of submitting a lump sum fee is that it provides a relatively inflexible form of remuneration. Percentage fees provide this flexibility, but, of course, they can decrease as well as increase with fluctuations in the scope of the project.

Spon's indicative fee scale (Method 2)

Indicative percentage fee scale: new works (+ external works)

Table 27

Construction cost (£)	Class 1 (%)	Class 2 (%)	Class 3 (%)	Class 4 (%)	Class 5 (%)
50,000	7.90	8.70	–	–	–
75,000	7.25	7.80	8.40	–	–
100,000	7.10	7.60	8.20	8.90	9.60
250,000	6.20	6.70	7.20	7.80	8.40
500,000	5.75	6.25	6.75	7.25	7.90
1,000,000	5.40	5.90	6.20	6.80	7.50
2,500,000	5.15	5.60	6.10	6.60	7.10
5,000,000	–	–	5.97	6.50	7.00
> 10,000,000	–	–	5.95	6.45	6.97

Indicative percentage fee scale: conversion

Table 28

Construction cost (£)	Class 1 (%)	Class 2 (%)	Class 3 (%)	Class 4 (%)	Class 5 (%)
50,000	11.60	12.60	–	–	–
75,000	10.70	11.60	12.40	–	–
100,000	10.40	11.30	12.20	13.15	14.10
250,000	9.30	10.10	10.85	11.75	12.55
500,000	8.70	9.45	10.20	11.05	11.80
1,000,000	8.25	9.00	9.70	10.55	11.30
2,500,000	–	–	9.25	10.00	10.75
5,000,000	–	–	9.10	9.85	10.55
> 10,000,000	–	–	9.00	9.75	1,045

Summary of results

Table 29

			Fee
7.10% of New works + external works 2,229,194 + 436,898 = 2,666,092			189,293
11.80% of Conversions	471,924		55,687
Contingencies (2.5%)	138,645	786,638	19,666
Furniture (2.5%)	452,983		
Incinerator (2.5%)	195,010		
Archaeology (1%)	19,700		197
Lump sum fee			**264,843**

Expressed as an overall percentage = 264,843/3,924,654 × 100 = **6.75%**

To use the professional indicators of fees, therefore, will produce similar results. Spon's figures are slightly higher than the RIBA indicative fees, but they do provide a useful comparison and give some confidence to the RIBA scale.

It is therefore a matter of commercial choice whether, in this instance, to quote 6.75% (Spon's) or 6.53% (RIBA) for the total works. The difference is only some £8,500 on approximately £4 million of construction works.

C Analytical estimating of fees

Introduction

Whilst the builders have been producing estimates and calculating building costs for over two centuries, the professions have simply charged a percentage fee on the final account of the builder. It has not been necessary to calculate fees or to keep any records of costs. This means that the architectural profession particularly has now to move very fast to provide databases of reliable information as a basis for fee bidding.

Fortunately, fee bidding for architects has arisen at a time when there is a rise in the development and use of computers. Computer-aided design (CAD) is now the norm in most professional offices, but computer-aided estimating (CAE) has still to be universally adopted. The extent to which manual methods are (at present) duplicated by CAE systems has prompted Potter and Scoins (1994) to argue that this has resulted in a 'tremendous loss of opportunity' as they see that little attempt has been made to 'consider the possibility and benefits of more productive ways of producing estimates offered by the computer' (Sher 1996).

This, however, should not deter the profession from embracing CAE, particularly for collecting, estimating and planning data for future bids. It is possible to have multiple CAE libraries reserved for different types of work and different levels of design complexities with, for example, different grades of staff. According to the CIOB *Code of Estimating Practice* (1997), 'the records of costs and outputs achieved on similar work from previous projects is a major source of information used in estimating'.

In all areas of risk assessment (and that is what a fee bid is), the big picture, the finished design, must be broken down into small units with which one is familiar. A joiner, for example, will not 'guesstimate' a price for a skirting board without considering the particular room in which it is going to be fixed. The room may be on the eleventh floor, there may be many mitres and stop ends, etc. The fixing cost of the skirting will therefore take all these unique factors into account as a job lot. By dividing the total cost by the quantity of skirting in the room, a price per linear metre can be obtained. To give a price for the skirting, as in this example by the room, as a lump sum would be little more than a wild guess; the joiner would reduce the risk by guessing a comfortably high figure.

Thompson (1997) extolled the architect to 'agree the terms of the appointment, together with details of the fees', although he did not offer any guidance on the calculation of fees except the use of a 'percentage of the cost of the project'. Blackwood *et al.* (1992) extended the discussion further by offering some preliminary conclusions to their research into fee bidding as:

- Because of the [then] widespread application of recommended fee scales, design managers were traditionally able to work from a linear fee to identify permissible resource requirements and ensure profitability through the application of comprehensive cost control systems.
- Planning and estimating of design work is still perceived by design professionals to be 'flying by the seat of the pants' activity and consequently empirical methods not supported by specific data, such as the number of

drawings or a broad comparison based on experience of similar projects, have been adopted to estimate design resources.

- Whilst most consultants recognized that in the [then] current competitive environment, a more rational approach should be adopted to planning and estimating resources for design work, and were considering changes, none of the companies were actively receiving their estimating systems.
- The design managers agreed that the data in their cost control system was not used directly to assist estimating, but most considered that the information could be of value.

Taking this argument into the present architectural profession, in order to reduce the risk to manageable and known features, the proposal of Blackwood et al. (1992) has been adopted here. The possible numbers of drawings in this example have been calculated and the cost of producing each drawing, together with other factors, such as office conditions and site management, added to produce an estimate of costs.

Methodology

The methodology is shown in the methodology diagram (Figure 16).

Estimates of office costs

Introduction

Using the figures supplied through consultation with the fictitious 'AB Architect's' partners, an accurate estimate of the running costs for the practice over the forthcoming year can be calculated. From this total, the average cost per man-year can be calculated. By working out the total man-days for each year, an average cost per man-day can be produced.

However, to increase the accuracy of the analytical method of fee bidding, a further breakdown of man-day costs will be performed. Each member of staff commands a different salary structure, has a different holiday provision and has other associated costs such as pensions and benefits. By calculating a more employee-specific cost per man-day and reflecting this in the man-days each employee type will spend on the practice involvement on the project, a more accurate analytical fee bid can be ascertained (Brooks 1998).

Both figures will be carried through the calculation process and comparisons and conclusions submitted. For the purpose of this exercise:

- call the average cost per man-day the practice wide figure (I); and
- call the average cost per employee type the employee-specific figure (II).

However, figures (I) and (II) are calculated using office cost totals that include a general figure for motoring expenses. The results for figures (III) and (IV) give a more accurate result, as they are calculated on a job-specific basis by removing the motoring expenses from the calculation (the motoring expenses will be added later as an additional factor to the project cost). Results for figures (III) and (IV) give the most accurate cost assessment and will, therefore, be carried forward into the final cost-calculation estimate.

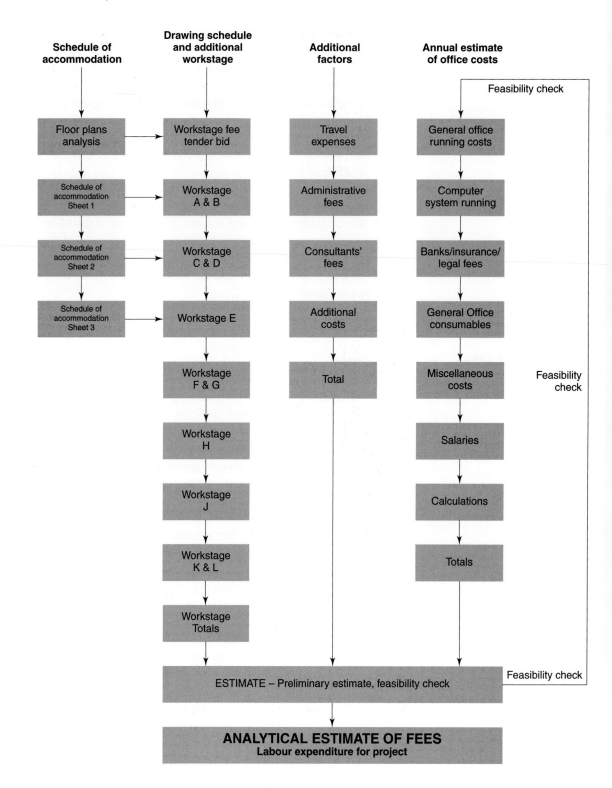

16 Methodology diagram

General office running costs

Table 30

Item	Cost (£)
Rent (£7.75/square foot)	15,500
Business rates	4,000
Electricity	1,000
Gas	1,500
Water rates	150
Office maintenance (including security)	3,000
Telephone	4,500
Total	29,650

Computer system running costs

Table 31

Item	Cost (£)
Computer equipment	6,000
Computer consumables	1,200
CAD training	1,750
Software updates	1,200
Internet/e-mail account (excluding calls)	240
Total	10,390

Banks/insurance/legal fees

Table 32

Item	Cost (£)
Bank charges	2,565
Bank interest (on potential overdraft)	2,050
Professional indemnity insurance (PII)	5,125
Accounts/legal fees	5,125
Insurance (office/third party)	1,025
Total	15,890

General office consumables

Table 33

Item	Cost (£)
Photocopier (rent and ink)	1,000
Photography (film and processing)	125
Office refreshments	600
Postage charges	350
Stationary	2,300
Office sundries	1,250
Magazines/technical literature	1,000
Total	6,625

Miscellaneous costs

Table 34

Item	Cost (£)
Advertising	1,000
Motoring expenses (20,000 miles @ £0.45/mile)	8,000
Printing costs	2,500
Total	11,500

Motoring expenses are chargeable to individual projects. Therefore, they will be calculated later.

Salaries

Table 35

Item	Cost (£)
Salaries (including staff costs)	150,000
Total	150,000

Office running costs total

Table 36

Item	Cost (£)
Item	Cost (£)
General office running costs	29,650
Computer system running costs	10,390
Banks/insurance/legal fees	15,890
General office consumables	6,625
Miscellaneous costs	11,500
Salaries	150,000
Total office running costs over forthcoming year	224,055
Total (less motoring expenses)	216,055

Calculations: practice wide figure (1) – all projects

To calculate the average cost per man-day (practice wide (1)):

Total cost per man-year = total office running cost/no. of staff = £224,055/7 = £32,008.

Therefore,
Average cost per man-day = total cost per man-year/no. of working days per year = £32,008/232 = £137.96

Note that for all calculations, working days/year are based upon eight Bank Holidays and 20 days' holiday per person.

Calculations: employee-specific figure (II) – all projects

Define the employee groups:

Table 37

Employee type 'A'	Salary scale (£) 'B'	Assumed salary (£) 'C'	Holiday allowance (days/year) 'D'	Percentage productive time (fee chargeable time) 'E'
Partner (P)	30,000–40,000	33,750	24	65
Architect (A)	20,000–25,000	22,500	22	100
Technician (T)	15,000–20,000	17,500	20	100
Administrative (Ad)	12,500–17,500	15,000	20	not applicable

To calculate the employee-specific cost per day, the following calculation is required. First, a total is devised for office running costs per employee per year (less salaries):

[Total running costs – total salaries (including administrative staff)]/productive staff members = (£224,055 – £150,000)/7 = £74,055/7 = £10,579.

The second step is to calculate each employee type's cost per person-day:

Assumed salary for specific employee type (C) = running costs per employee per year/total annual working days (D) = (C + 10,579.28)/D.

Table 38

Employee type 'A'	Assumed salary (£) 'C'	Holiday allowance (days/year) 'D'	Calculation $\dfrac{(C + 10,579.28)}{260 - (D + 8)^*}$	Employee-specific costs (£/day) 'E'
Partner (P)	33,750	24 + 8	$\dfrac{33,750 + 10,579}{228}$	194.42 (E1)
Architect (A)	22,500	22 + 8	$\dfrac{22,500 + 10,579}{230}$	143.82 (E2)
Technician (T)	17,500	20 + 8	$\dfrac{17,500 + 10,579}{232}$	121.03 (E3)
Secretary (S)	15,000	20 + 8	$\dfrac{15,000 + 10,579}{232}$	110.25 (E4)

Assuming 260 working days per year and eight days Bank Holiday.

Therefore:
Average cost per man-day (practice wide (I)) = **£137.96**

Employee-specific cost per day (practice wide (II)) (Table 37) = **£110.25 to £194.42**.

Check and compare average figures for each method:

$$(2 \times P \times E1) + (1 \times A \times E2) + (3 \times T \times E3)/6 = £895.75/6 = £149.29.$$

Note the minor variation in figures are due to the different holiday provisions for (I) and (II).

Calculations: practice wide figure (III) – job specific

Revised figure for total office running cost = total office running costs – motoring expenses = £224,055 – £8,000 = **£216,055**

To calculate the average cost per man-day (III):

Total cost per man-year = total office running cost/no. of productive staff = £216,055/7 = £30,865.

Therefore,

Average cost per man-day = total cost per man-year/no. of working days per year = £30,865/232 = **£133.04**.

Calculations: employee-specific figure (IV) – job specific

To calculate the employee-specific cost per day, the following calculation is required. First, a total is devised for office running costs per employee per year (less salaries):

[Total running costs (revised) – total salaries (including administrative staff)]/productive staff members

$$= (£216,055 – £150,000)/7 = £66,055/7 = £9,436.40.$$

The second step is to calculate each employee type's cost per person-day:

Assumed salary for specific employee type (C) = running costs per employee per year/total annual working days (D) = (C + 9,436.4)/D.

Table 39

Employee type type 'A'	Assumed salary (£) C	Holiday allowance (days/year) 'D'	Calculation $\dfrac{(C + 9,436.4)}{260 - (D + 8)^*}$	Employee-specific costs (£/day) 'E'
Partner (P)	33,750	24	$\dfrac{33,750 + 9,436.4}{228}$	189.41 (E1)
Architect (A)	22,500	22	$\dfrac{22,500 + 9,436.4}{230}$	138.85 (E2)
Technician (T)	17,500	20	$\dfrac{17,500 + 9,436.4}{232}$	116.10 (E3)
Secretary (S)	15,000	20	$\dfrac{15,000 + 9,436.4}{232}$	105.32 (E4)

Assuming 260 working days per year and eight days Bank Holiday.

Therefore:

Average cost per man-day (practice wide (III)) – job specific = **£133.04**

Employee-specific cost per day (practice wide (IV)) – job specific (Table 39) = **£105.32 to £189.41**.

Summary of results
Average cost per man-day (practice wide figure (I)) = **£137.96**
Employee-specific cost per day (practice wide figure (II)) = **£110.25 to £194.42**
Average cost per man-day (practice wide figure (III)) – job specific = **£133.04**
Employee-specific cost per day (practice wide figure (IV)) – job specific = **£105.32 to £189.41**.

Schedule of accommodation

Ground-floor plan

The ground-floor plan is shown in Figure 17.

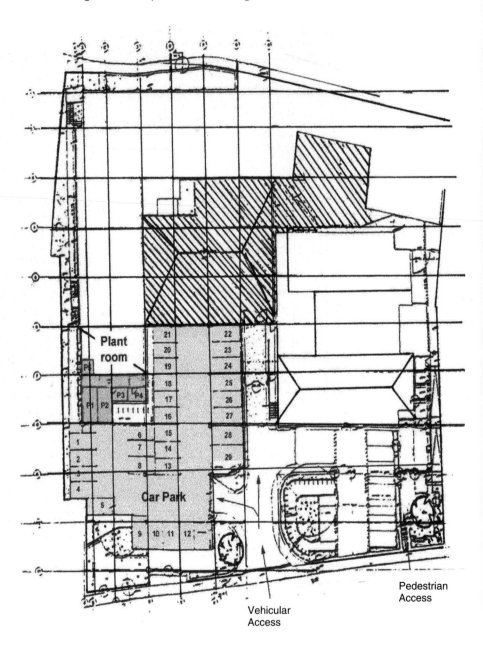

Plant room

Car Park

Pedestrian Access

Vehicular Access

17 Ground-floor plan

First-floor plan

The first-floor plan is shown in Figure 18.

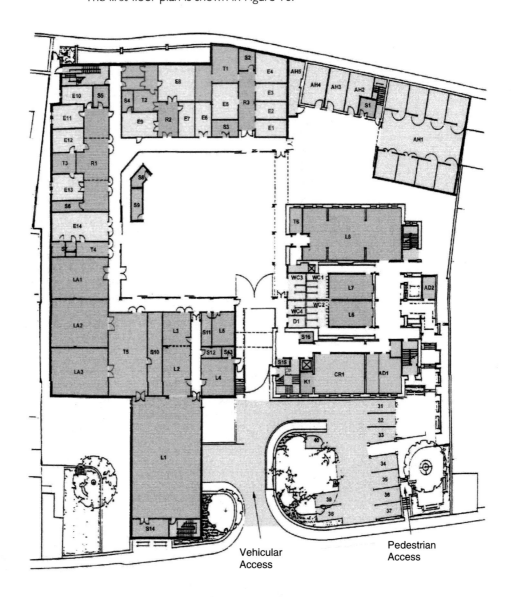

18 First-floor plan

Second-floor plan

The second-floor plan is shown in Figure 19.

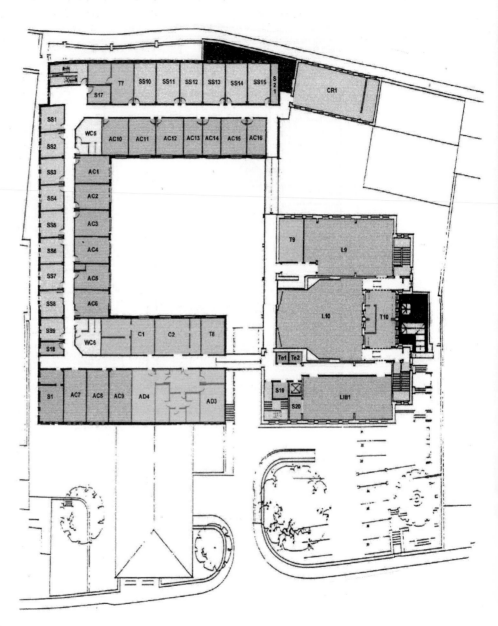

19 Second-floor plan

Schedule of accommodation (Sheet 1)

Table 40

Room type	Room number	New build (N) or conversion (C)	Fit-out level	Specialist subcontractor
Storage areas	AH1	C	A	
	AH2	C	A	
	AH3	C	A	
	AH4	C	A	
	AH5	C	A	
Examination rooms	E1	N	H	
	E2	N	H	
	E3	N	H	
	E4	N	H	
	E5	N	H	
	E6	N	H	
	E7	N	H	
	E8	N	H	
	E9	N	H	
	E10	N	H	
	E11	N	H	
	E12	N	H	
	E13	N	H	
	E14	N	H	
Recovery/preparation rooms	R1	N	H	
	R2	N	H	
	R3	N	H	
Laboratories	LA1	N	L	LF, LFC/E, CN
	LA2	N	L	LF, LFC/E, CN
	LA3	N	L	LF, LFC/E, CN
Lecture/seminar rooms	L1	N	Se	AV, CN
	L2	N	Se	AV, CN
	L3	N	Se	AV, CN
	L4	N	Se	AV, CN
	L5	N	Se	AV, CN
	L6	C	Se	AV, CN
	L7	C	Se	AV, CN
	L8	C	Se	AV, CN
	L9	C	Se	AV, CN
	L10	C	Se	AV, CN
Technical support rooms	T1	N	T	
	T2	N	T	
	T3	N	T	
	T4	N	T	
	T5	N	T	
	T6	C	T	
	T7	N	T	
	T8	N	T	
	T9	C	T	
	T10	C	T	

Schedule of accommodation (Sheet 2)

Table 41

Room type	Room number	New build (N) or conversion (C)	Fit-out level	Specialist subcontractor
Student study room	SS1	N	S	CN
	SS2	N	S	CN
	SS3	N	S	CN
	SS4	N	S	CN
	SS5	N	S	CN
	SS6	N	S	CN
	SS7	N	S	CN
	SS8	N	S	CN
	SS9	N	S	CN
	SS10	N	S	CN
	SS11	N	S	CN
	SS12	N	S	CN
	SS13	N	S	CN
	SS14	N	S	CN
	SS15	N	S	CN
Computer rooms	C1	N	Co	CN
	C2	N	Co	CN
Academic offices	AC1	N	O	CN
	AC2	N	O	CN
	AC3	N	O	CN
	AC4	N	O	CN
	AC5	N	O	CN
	AC6	N	O	CN
	AC7	N	O	CN
	AC8	N	O	CN
	AC9	N	O	CN
	AC10	N	O	CN
	AC11	N	O	CN
	AC12	N	O	CN
	AC13	N	O	CN
	AC14	N	O	CN
	AC15	N	O	CN
	AC16	N	O	CN
Library	Lib1	C	O	CN
Common rooms	CR1	C	C	
	CR2	N	C	
Kitchen	K1	C	K	
Administrative rooms	AD1	C	O	CN
	AD2	C	O	CN
	AD3	N	O	CN
	AD4	N	O	CN
Public telephone booths	Te1	C	Te	
	Te2	C	Te	
Staff room	ST1	C	C	

Schedule of Accommodation (Sheet 3)

Table 42

Room type	Room number	New build (N) or conversion (C)	Fit-out level	Specialist subcontractor
Toilets	WC1	C	H	
	WC2	C	H	
	WC3	C	H	
	WC4	C	H	
	WC5	N	H	
	WC6	N	H	
Storage/service rooms	S1	C	So	
	S2	N	So	
	S3	N	So	
	S4	N	So	
	S5	N	So	
	S6	N	So	
	S7	N	So	
	S8	N	So	
	S9	N	So	
	S10	N	So	
	S11	N	So	
	S12	N	So	
	S13	N	So	
	S14	N	So	
	S15	C	So	
	S16	C	So	
	S17	C	So	
	S18	C	So	
	S19	C	So	
	S20	C	So	
Plant room	P1	N	P	
	P2	N	P	
	P3	N	P	
	P4	N	P	

Drawing schedule and additional workstage requirements

Workstage: fee-bid tender proposal

Table 43 shows the presentation drawings to submit with a fee bid.

Table 43

Draw no. 0011	Drawing title	Type	Size	Scale	Original time allowance (days) P	A	T	No. of revs	Revision time allowance (days) P	A	T
001	Site Location Plan	C, V	A3	1:1,250			2	0			
002	Site Plan	C, V	A3	1:500			2	0			
003	North Elevation	C, V	A3	1:200			2	0			
004	East Elevation	C, V	A3	1:200			2	0			
005	South Elevation	C, V	A3	1:200			2	0			
006	West Elevation	C, V	A3	1:200			2	0			
007	Preliminary Perspective	C, V	A3	Nts	2						
Total						2	12				

As part of the fee-bid tender package produced by the practice, a full set of presentation drawings would be compiled to illustrate and expand upon the proposal. This procedure is used to show a commitment by the firm to the project at an early stage. The following schedule lists these drawings. However, the time allotted for these will not be included in the final calculation of the total office time expended as these drawings are absorbed into the office costs of producing fee-bid submissions.

Workstages A. Inception and B. Feasibility

The bulk of this stage of work has already been completed by the consultants who conducted the original feasibility study and outline proposal for the client. However, a certain number of 'as existing' drawings will be required to cover these stages of the project to act as templates for proceeding drawings, for submissions to the local authority and for archiving. Table 44 shows the drawings completed on receipt of a full building survey from the consultant surveyors.

Table 44

Draw no. 0011	Drawing title	Type	Size	Scale	Original time allowance (days) P	A	T	No. of revs	Revision time allowance (days) P	A	T
100	As Existing Site Location Plan/Site plan	L	A1	1:1,250 1:500			1.5	0			
101	As exist. GF plan	L	A1	1:100			1.5	0			
102	As exist. FF plan	L	A1	1:100			1.5	0			
103	As exist. SF plan	L	A1	1:100			1.5	0			
104	As exist. Elevation A	L	A1	1:100			1.5	0			
105	As exist. Elevation B	L	A1	1:100			1.5	0			
106	As exist. Elevation C	L	A1	1:100			1.5	0			
107	As exist. Elevation D	L	A1	1:100			1.5	0			
108	As exist. Section A–A	L	A1	1:100			1.5	0			
109	As exist. Section B–B	L	A1	1:100			1.5	0			
110	As exist. Section C–C	L	A1	1:100			1,5	0			
111	As exist. Section D–D	L	A1	1:100			1.5	0			
Total							18				

Additional workstages' requirements

Table 45

Description	Travel to site required (Y/N)	Time allowance (days)		
		P	A	T
Office programming meeting (1)	N	0.5	0.5	0.5
Client meeting (1) on site	Y	1	1	
Site appraisal including photographic study	Y		1	1
Site feasibility study	N		2	
Consultation with surveyors	N		0.25	
Quantity surveyors meeting (1)	N		0.5	
Miscellaneous project time	N	3	1	
Totals	2	4.5	6.25	1.5

Table 46

Totals for Workstages A and B	Travel to site	Time allowance (days)		
		P	A	T
Employee-specific total	2 (car journeys)	4.5	6.25	18.5
Total for practice	4 (person journeys)	**29.25**		

Workstage C. Outline proposals

The stage comments (as defined by RIBA) are:

To determine general approach to layout, design and construction in order to obtain authoritative approval of the client on the outline proposals and accompanying report. . . . Develop the brief further. Carry out studies on user requirements, technical problems, planning, design and costs, as necessary to reach decisions.

Table 47

Draw no. 0011	Drawing title	Type	Size	Scale	Original time allowance (days) P	A	T	No. of revs	Revision time allowance (days) P	A	T
201	As prop. Site location plan/Site plan	L	A1	1:1,250 1:500			2	1			1
202	As prop. GF plan	L	A1	1:100			2	1			1
203	As prop. FF plan	L	A1	1:100			2	1			1
204	As prop. SF plan	L	A1	1:100			2	1			1
205	As prop. Roof plan	L	A1	1:100			2	1			1
206	As prop. Elevation A	L	A1	1:100			2	1			1
207	As prop. Elevation B	L	A1	1:100			2	1			1
208	As prop. Elevation C	L	A1	1:100			2	1			1
209	As prop. Elevation D	L	A1	1:100			2	1			1
210	As prop. Elevation E	L	A1	1:100			2	1			1
211	As Prop. Elevation F	L	A1	1:100			2	1			1
212	As Prop. Elevation G	L	A1	1:100			2	1			1
213	As Prop. Elevation H	L	A1	1:100			2	1			1
214	As prop. Section A–A	L	A1	1:100			2	1			1
215	As prop. Section B–B	L	A1	1:100			2	1			1
216	As prop. Section C–C	L	A1	1:100			2	1			1
217	As prop. Section D–D	L	A1	1:100			2	1			1
218	As prop. Elevations A & B	C, V	A3	Nts		2	2	1			1
219	As prop. Elevations C & D	C, V	A3	Nts		2	2	1			1
220	3D models views 1	C, V	A3	Nts		2	2	0			
221	3D models views 2	C, V	A3	Nts		2	2	0			
Totals					0	8	42		0	0	19

Additional workstage requirements

Table 48

Description	Travel to site required (Y/N)	Time allowance (days) P	A	T
Office programming meeting (2)	N	0.25	0.25	0.25
Scheme redesign	N	2	7	2
Client meeting (2) on site	Y	1	1	
Client meeting (3) at office	N	0.5	0.5	
Consultation with QS	N		0.5	
Consultation with planning authority	N		1	
Miscellaneous project time	N	3	1	
Totals	1	6.75	11.25	2.25

Table 49

Totals for Workstages C	Travel to site	Time allowance (days)		
		P	A	T
Employee-specific totals	1 (car journeys)	6.75	19.25	63.25
Total for practice	2 (person journeys)		**89.25**	

Workstage D. Scheme design

The stage comments (as defined by RIBA) are:

To complete the brief and decide on particular proposals, including planning arrangement appearance, constructional method, outline specification, and cost, and to obtain all approvals. . . . Final development of the brief, full design of the project by architect, preliminary design by engineers, preparation of cost plan and full explanatory report. Submission of proposals for all approvals.

Table 50

Draw no. 0011	Drawing title	Type	Size	Scale	Original time allowance (days)			No. of revs	Revision time allowance (days)		
					P	A	T		P	A	T
201	As prop. Site location plan/Site plan	L	A1	1:1,250 1:500		1	1			1	
202	As prop. GF plan	L	A1	1:100		1	1			1	
203	As prop. FF plan	L	A1	1:100		1	1			1	
204	As prop. SF plan	L	A1	1:100		1	1			1	
205	As prop. Roof plan	L	A1	1:100		1	1			1	
206	As prop. Elevation A	L	A1	1:100		1	1			1	
207	As prop. Elevation B	L	A1	1:100		1	1			1	
208	As prop. Elevation C	L	A1	1:100		1	1			1	
209	As prop. Elevation D	L	A1	1:100		1	1			1	
210	As prop. Elevation E	L	A1	1:100		1	1			1	
211	As Prop. Elevation F	L	A1	1:100		1	1			1	
212	As Prop. Elevation G	L	A1	1:100		1	1			1	
213	As Prop. Elevation H	L	A1	1:100		1	1			1	
214	As prop. Section A–A	L	A1	1:100		1	1			1	
215	As prop. Section B–B	L	A1	1:100		1	1			1	
216	As prop. Section C–C	L	A1	1:100		1	1			1	
217	As prop. Section D–D	L	A1	1:100		1	1			1	
218	As prop. Elevations A & B	C, V	A3	Nts		2	1			1	
219	As prop. Elevations C & D	C, V	A3	Nts		2	1			1	
220	3D models views 1	C, V	A3	Nts	1	1	0				
221	3D models views 2	C, V	A3	Nts	1	1	0				
222	Landscaping scheme	L	A1	1:500	1		1			1	
223	Ext. Finishes Board 1	C	A2	Nts	1	1	1			0.5	
224	Ext. Finishes Board 2	C	A2	Nts	1	1	1			0.5	
Totals					0	5	25		0	0	21

Copies of drawings are archived as hard and digital copy as the planning application set.

Additional workstage requirements

Table 51

Description	Travel to site required (Y/N)	Time allowance (days)		
		P	A	T
Office programming meeting 3	N	0.25	0.25	0.25
Scheme design	N	1	4	1
Client meeting (4) on site	Y	1	1	
Client meeting (5) at office	N	0.5	0.5	
Consultation with QS	N		1	
Consultation with planning authority (PA)	N		3	
Meeting with PA 1	Y	1	1	
Meeting with PA 2	Y		1	
Consultation with PA conservation officer (CO)	N		0.5	
Consultation with PA fire officer (FO)	N		0.5	
Consultation with PA highway officer (HO)	N		0.5	
Consultation with structural engineer	N		1	
Meeting with structural engineer (at office)	N		0.5	
Consultation with PA building control officer	N		0.5	
Consultation with service providers (telephone, gas, electricity, etc.)	N		0.5	
Administration work for planning application	N		2	
Client meeting (6) at office	N		0.5	
Planning application submission to PA	N		0.5	
CDM administration	N		0.25	
Miscellaneous project time	N	3	1	
Totals	3	6.75	20	1.25

Table 52

Totals for Workstages D	Travel to site	Time allowance (days)		
		P	A	T
Employee-specific totals	3 (car journeys)	3.75	25	47.25
Total for practice	5 (person journeys)	**76**		

Workstage E. Detail design

The stage comments (as defined by RIBA) are:

To obtain final decision on every matter related to design, specification, construction and cost. . . . Full design of every part and component of the building by collaboration of all concerned. Complete cost checking of designs.

Table 53

Draw no. 0011	Drawing title	Type	Size	Scale	Original time allowance (days)			No. of revs	Revision time allowance (days)		
					P	A	T		P	A	T
201	Site location plan/Site plan	L	A1	1:1,250 1:500							
202	GF plan	L	A1	1:100			2	1			1
203	FF plan	L	A1	1:100			2	1			1
204	SF plan	L	A1	1:100			2	1			1
205	Roof plan	L	A1	1:100			2	1			1
206	Elevation A	L	A1	1:100			2	1			1
207	Elevation B	L	A1	1:100			2	1			1
208	Elevation C	L	A1	1:100			2	1			1
209	Elevation D	L	A1	1:100			2	1			1
210	Elevation E	L	A1	1:100			1	1			1
211	Elevation F	L	A1	1:100			1	1			1
212	Elevation G	L	A1	1:100			1	1			1
213	Elevation H	L	A1	1:100			1	1			1
214	Section A–A	L	A1	1:100			2	1			1
215	Section B–B	L	A1	1:100			2	1			1
216	Section C–C	L	A1	1:100			2	1			1
217	Section D–D	L	A1	1:100			2	1			1
218	Elevations A & B	C, V	A3	Nts							
219	Elevations C & D	C, V	A3	Nts							
220	3D models views 1	C, V	A3	Nts							
221	3D models views 2	C, V	A3	Nts							
222	Landscaping scheme	L	A1	1:500							
223	Ext. Finishes Board 1	C	A2	Nts							
224	Ext. Finishes Board 2	C	A2	Nts							
Totals					0	0	28		0	0	16

For building regulations' application, the relevant details are added to the existing plan/section/elevation drawings and the alterations noted in revision comments. Copies of the drawings are archived as hard and digital copy as the building regulations' set.

Additional workstage requirements

Table 54

Description	Travel to site required (Y/N)	Time allowance (days)		
		P	A	T
Office programming meeting (4)	N		0.25	0.25
Potential planning application redesign (x)*	N	x	x	x
General scheme design	N	0.25	2	1
Client meeting (5) on site	Y	1	1	
Consultation with QS	N		1	
Consultation with planning authority (PA)	N		1	
Consultation with PA conservation officer (CO)	N		0.25	
Consultation with PA fire officer (FO)	N		0.25	
Consultation with PA highway officer (HO)	N		0.25	
Consultation with structural engineer	N		2	
Meeting with structural engineer (2)	N		0.5	
Consultation with PA building control officer	N		2	
Detailed design work for building register application	N		4	
Administration work for building register application	N		1	
Building register application to building control	N		0.5	
Miscellaneous project time	N	3	1	
Totals	1	4.25	17	1.25

*Potential planning application redesign and administrative work (factor x): although all stages are completed and the relevant bodies consulted before the planning application, the actual receipt of consent is an unknown factor. The planning authority and the relevant local group need to be sounded out at a very early stage to account for any unseen extensions to the precontract programme. The assumption for this exercise is that any major concerns of the planning authority were dealt with during the consultation period before the planning application was lodged and full consent was gained within the normal time frame (including an allowance for the scheme to go to committee).

Table 55

Totals for Workstages E	Travel to site	Time allowance (days)		
		P	A	T
Employee-specific totals	1 (car journeys)	4.25	17	45.25
Total for practice	2 (person journeys)		**66.5**	

Workstages F. Production information and G. Bills of quantity

The stage comments (as defined by RIBA) are:

[Stage F] To prepare production information and make final detailed decisions to carry out work. . . . Preparation of final production information i.e. drawings, schedules and specifications.

[Stage G] To prepare and complete all information and arrangements for obtaining tender. . . . Preparation of Bills of Quantities and tender documents.

Table 56

Draw no. 0011	Drawing title	Type	Size	Scale	P	A	T	No. of revs	P	A	T
					Original time allowance (days)				Revision time allowance (days)		
202	GF plan	L	A1	1:100			0.2				
203	FF plan	L	A1	1:100			0.2				
204	SF plan	L	A1	1:100			0.2				
205	Roof plan	L	A1	1:100			0.2				
206	Elevation A	L	A1	1:100			0.2				
207	Elevation B	L	A1	1:100			0.2				
208	Elevation C	L	A1	1:100			0.2				
209	Elevation D	L	A1	1:100			0.2				
210	Elevation E	L	A1	1:100			0.2				
211	Elevation F	L	A1	1:100			0.2				
212	Elevation G	L	A1	1:100			0.2				
213	Elevation H	L	A1	1:100			0.2				
214	Section A–A	L	A1	1:100			0.2				
215	Section B–B	L	A1	1:100			0.2				
216	Section C–C	L	A1	1:100			0.2				
217	Section D–D	L	A1	1:100			0.2				
225	Foundation plan	L	A1	1:100			2	1			1
226	Fire strategy plan (all floors)	L	A0	1:200			2	1			1
227	Ventilation strategy plan (all floors)	L	A0	1:200			3	1			1
228	Heating plan (all floors)	L	A0	1:200			3	1			1
229	Drainage plan	L	A0	1:200			3	1			1
230	Ceiling grid layout (all floors)	L	A0	1:200			3	1			1
231	Electrical layout plan (all floors)	L	A0	1:200			3	1			1
232	Disabled Access strategy	L	A1	1:100			3	1			1
233	Rooms AH1-AH5. Typical arrang. & spec	L	A1	1:50			3				
234	Rooms E1-E14 Typical arrang. & spec	L	A1	1:50			3				
235	Rooms R1-R3 Typical arrang. & spec	L	A1	1:50			3				
236	Rooms LA1-LA3 Typical arrang. & spec	L	A1	1:50			3				
237	Rooms L1-L10 Typical arrang. & spec	L	A1	1:50			3				
238	Rooms T1-T10 Typical arrang. & spec	L	A1	1:50			3				
239	Rooms SS1-SS15 Typical arrang. & spec	L	A1	1:50			3				

Table 56 cont.

Draw no. 0011/	Drawing title	Type	Size	Scale	Original time allowance (days)			No. of revs	Revision time allowance (days)		
					P	A	T		P	A	T
240	Rooms C1 & C2 Typical arrang. & spec	L	A1	1:50			3				
241	Rooms AC1 – AC16 Typical arrang. & spec	L	A1	1:50			3				
242	Room LIB1 Typical arrang. & spec	L	A1	1:50			3				
243	Rooms CR1 & CR2 Typical arrang. & spec	L	A1	1:50			3				
244	Room K1 Typical arrang. & spec	L	A1	1:50			3				
245	Rooms AD1 – AD4 Typical arrang. & spec	L	A1	1:50			3				
246	Rooms Te1 & Te2 Typical arrang. & spec	L	A1	1:50			3				
247	Room ST1 Typical arrang. & spec	L	A1	1:50			3				
248	Room WC1 – WC6 Typical arrang. & spec	L	A1	1:50			3				
249	Room S1 – S20 Typical arrang. & spec	L	A1	1:50			3				
250	Room P1 – P4 Typical arrang. & spec	L	A1	1:50			3				
251	Detail sheet A: Foundations	L	A1	1:5, 1:10			3	I			I
252	Detail sheet B: Ext. Walls	L	A1	1:5, 1:10			5	I			I
253	Detail sheet C: Int. Walls	L	A1	1:5, 1:10			3	I			I
254	Detail sheet D: Windows	L	A1	1:5, 1:10			5	I			I
255	Detail sheet E: Doors	L	A1	1:5, 1:10			3	I			I
256	Detail sheet F: Roof	L	A1	1:5, 1:10			3	I			I
257	Detail sheet G: Stairs	L	A1	1:5, 1:10			4	I			I
258	Detail sheet H: Lifts	L	A1	1:5, 1:10			3	I			I
259	Detail sheet J: WCs	L	A1	1:5, 1:10			4	I			I
260	Detail sheet K: New & conversion interface, sheet 1	L	A1	1:5, 1:10			4	I			I
261	Detail sheet K: New & conversion interface, sheet 2	L	A1	1:5, 1:10			4	I			I
300	Schedule A: Doors	D	A3 X5	Nts			7	I			I
301	Schedule B: Windows	D	A3 X5	Nts			7	I			I
302	Schedule C: Ironmongery	D	A3 X5	Nts			7	I			I
303	Schedule D: Finishes	D	A3 X5	Nts			7	I			I
304	Schedule E: Sanitary	D	A3 X5	Nts			7	I			I
305	Schedule F: Manholes	D	A3 X2	Nts			7	I			I

Table 56 cont.

Draw no. 0011	Drawing title	Type	Size	Scale	Original time allowance (days)			No. of revs	Revision time allowance (days)		
					P	A	T		P	A	T
400	Specification Doc. 1: Tendering particulars	D	A4	Nts		+					
401	Specification Doc. 2: Preliminaries	D	A4	Nts		+					
402	Specification Doc. 3: Demolitions & alterations	D	A4	Nts		+					
403	Specification Doc. 4: Excavation & Earthworks	D	A4	Nts		+					
404	Specification Doc. 5: Piling	D	A4	Nts		+					
405	Specification Doc. 6: Concrete work	D	A4	Nts		+					
406	Specification Doc. 7: Brickwork & Blockwork	D	A4	Nts		+					
407	Specification Doc. 8: Underpinning	D	A4	Nts		+					
408	Specification Doc. 9: Rubble walling	D	A4	Nts		+					
409	Specification Doc. 10: Masonry	D	A4	Nts		+					
410	Specification Doc. 11: Asphalt work	D	A4	Nts		+					
411	Specification Doc. 12: Roofing	D	A4	Nts		+					
412	Specification Doc. 13: Woodwork	D	A4	Nts		+					
413	Specification Doc. 14: Structural steelwork	D	A4	Nts		+					
414	Specification Doc. 15: Metalwork	D	A4	Nts		+					
415	Specification Doc. 16: Plumbing and mech. engin. installations	D	A4	Nts		+					
416	Specification Doc. 17: Elect. installation	D	A4	Nts		+					
417	Specification Doc. 18: Services general	D	A4	Nts		+					
418	Specification Doc. 19: Floor, wall and ceiling finishes	D	A4	Nts		+					
419	Specification Doc. 20: Glazing	D	A4	Nts		+					
420	Specification Doc. 21: Painting & decorating	D	A4	Nts		+					
421	Specification Doc. 22: Drainage	D	A4	Nts		+					
422	Specification Doc. 23: External works & fencing	D	A4	Nts		+					
	Specification document: 25 days total for A (architect).										
501	CDM file	D	A4	Nts	5						

Additional workstages' requirements

Table 57

Description	Travel to site required (Y/N)	Time allowance (days)		
		P	A	T
Office programming meeting (5)	N		0.25	0.25
General scheme design	N	0.25	2	1
Client meeting (6) on site	Y	1	1	
Consultation with QS	N		1	
Preparation of bill of quantities	N		2.5	
Consultation with structural engineer	N		1	
Meeting with structural engineer (3)	N		0.25	
Client meeting (7) at office	N		0.25	
Detailed design work for working drawings	N		3	2
Administration work for building register application	N		1	
Miscellaneous project time	N	4	1	
Totals	1	5.25	13.25	3.25

Table 58

Totals for Workstages F and G	Travel to site	Time allowance (days)		
		P	A	T
Employee-specific totals	1 (car journey)	5.25	43.25	191.25
Total for practice	2 (person journeys)	**239.75**		

Workstage H. Tender action

The stage comments (as defined by RIBA) are:

Action as recommended in NJCC Code of Procedure for single stage selective tendering.

No additional drawings are required for this stage. The tender package drawings are identified and archived.

Additional workstage requirements

Table 59

Description	Travel to site required (Y/N)	Time allowance (days)		
		P	A	T
Tender package administration.	N		2	
Tender bid assessment	N		2	
Consulations with client	N		2	
Client meeting (8) on site	Y		1	
Contract documentation preparation	N		1	
CDM risk assessments	N		1	
Precontract meeting (on site) with all relevant parties (contractor, client subcontractors)	Y		1	
Miscellaneous project time	N	3	1	
Total	2 (car journeys)		3	11
Total for practice	2 (person journeys)	**14**		

Workstage J. Project planning

The stage comments (as defined by RIBA) are:

To enable the contractor to programme the work in accordance with contract conditions; brief site inspectorate; and make arrangements to commence work on-site.

There are no additional drawings required for this stage.

Additional workstage requirements

Table 60

Description	Travel to site required (Y/N)	Time allowance (days)		
		P	A	T
Client meeting (9) on site	Y		1	
Main contractor meeting (1) on site	Y		1	
Client meeting (10) on site	Y	1	1	
Main contractor programme assessment	N		1	
Main contractor meeting (2) on site	Y		1	
Miscellaneous project time	N	2	3	
Total	4 (car journeys)		3	8
Total for practice	5 (person journeys)	**11**		

Workstage K. Operations on site

The stage comments (as defined by RIBA) are:

To follow plans through to practical completion of the building.

There are no additional drawings required for this stage.

Additional workstage requirements

Table 61

Description	Travel to site required (Y/N)	Time allowance (days)		
		P	A	T
Further 20 site visits and inspections	Y		20	
Miscellaneous project time	N		10	
Drawing alteration/reissues	N			7
Contract administration work	N	3	7	
Totals	20 (car journeys)	3	37	7
Total for practice	20 (person journeys)		**47**	

Workstages L. Completion and M. Feedback

The stage comments (as defined by RIBA) are:

[Stage L] To hand over the building to the client for occupation, remedy any defects, settle the final account, and complete all works in accordance with the contract.

[Stage M] To analyse the management, construction and performance of the project. . . . Analysis of job records. Inspections of completed building. Studies of the building in use.

There are no additional drawings required for this stage.

Additional workstages' requirements

Table 62

Description	Travel to site required (Y/N)	Time allowance (days)		
		P	A	T
Preparation of maintenance manual	N			3
Miscellaneous project time	N	2	2	
Defects visits	Y		2	
Totals	2 (car journeys)	2	4	3
Total for practice	2 (person journeys)		**9**	

Workstage totals

Table 63

Project stage	Travel visits to site	Time allowance (days)		
		P	A	T
A. Inception and B. Feasibility	2	4.5	6.25	18.5
C. Outline proposals	1	6.75	19.25	63.25
D. Scheme design	3	6.75	25	47.25
E. Detail design	1	4.25	17	45.25
F. Production information and G. Bills of quantities	1	5.25	43.25	191.25
H. Tender action	2	3	11	
J. Project planning	4	3	8	
K. Operations on site	20	3	37	7
L. Completion and M. Feedback	2	2	4	3
Employee-specific total	36	38.5	170.75	375.5
Practice total (days)			**584**	
Practice total (hours)			**4,386**	

Checking consultants' and trade contractors' drawings

Table 64

Consultant	Building element	No. of drawings	Time allowance (4 days per drawing × 0.25%)	Total
Mechanical engineer	ventilation	6		
	fire system	3		
	boiler	1		
	ventilation: lecture halls	3		
	extraction: laboratories	3		
	schedules	3		19
Electrical engineer	general arrangement plans	6		
	room layouts	20		
	switch room	2		
	schedules	2		30
Structural engineer	general arrangement plans	6		
	reinforcement details	3		
	roof details	4		
	general details	3		16
Specialist laboratory subcontractor	laboratory furniture layouts	3		
	fume cupboards layout	1		
	general details	1		5
				=21
Trade contractors	joinery: laboratory benches	6		
	X-ray equipment	2		
	refrigeration	2		
	operating theatre equipment	8		
	security systems	3		21
Lifts	general plans	3		
	details	1		
	schedules	1		5
				96
				(say 100)

If four drawings can be checked a day, allow 25 days for checking the consultants' and specialists' drawings = 25 × 7.5 hours = **187.50 hours**.

Additional factors

Transport costs

By car:

Total number of car journeys (for up to four staff members) = 36
Distance for round trip = 300 miles
Cost @ £0.45/mile.

Therefore:
Total number of journeys × distance (miles) × cost/mile = 36 × 300 × 45 = **£4,860**.

By train:

Total number of person journeys = 44
Low estimate: return cost (off peak, Monday–Friday) = £39.50
High estimate: return cost (peak times, Monday–Friday) = £70.00

Therefore:
Low estimate = total number of person journeys × return cost (off peak, Monday–Friday) = 44 × 39.50 = £1,738

High estimate = total number of person journeys × return cost (peak times, Monday–Friday) = 44 × 70 = £3,080.

Therefore:
Average estimate for travel to site by train =

(Low estimate + high estimate)/2 = (1,738 + 3,080)/2 = £2,409.

The distance from the site to the train station is unknown. Therefore, at £10 per taxi fare per trip = 36 × 10 = £360.

Therefore:
Total cost for travel by train = **£2,769**

Comparing the two modes of transport, the train has a clear advantage in a basis comparison of costs assuming that 50% of meetings are scheduled for the late morning to take advantage of the reduced off-peak fares. Congestion rates for car travel and delays for train transport are unknown factors and thus effectively cancel each other out.

Therefore:
Total cost of travel to site for inspections and meetings = **£2,769**.

Administrative fees

Administration and non-productive time associated with the project carried out by the design and drafting team in the office has already been calculated for each workstage. However, this does not account for secretarial input into the project. Table 65 attempts to quantify this input.

Table 65

Project stage	Time allowance (days): secretary
A. Inception and B. Feasibility	2
C. Outline proposals	2
D. Scheme design	4
E. Detail design	4
F. Production information and G. Bills of quantities	4
H. Tender action	6
J. Project planning	2
K. Operations on site	4
L. Completion and M. Feedback	2
Total	**30**

It would be more usual to discount secretarial and administrative staff at this stage and include these costs within the overheads. However, if charges could be identified that are contract specific, then they can be calculated here.

Consultants' fees

The majority of consultants' fees would be paid directly by the client under the conditions agreed at the inception of the project (it is important that the client directly employs consultants to protect the architect from claims arising from their non-performance). The costs for the site survey and existing building survey should be covered by the practice and therefore must be included in the cost estimate:

- Full-site survey fee: £5,650
- Full survey of the existing building: £7,550.

Total (based on an estimate from surveying practice) =
£5,650 + £7,550 = £13,200.

Therefore:
Total charge for survey information to be added to estimate = **£13,200**.

Drawing revisions

In a recent research project, five sites were studied to ascertain the number of drawings that had to be revised and reissued. Figure 20 separates the design team from the trade contractor reissues for the various jobs. No details are available to discover the reasons for the changes – they may be mistakes on the part of the designers or changes in the client's brief. Whatever the causal factors, reissues are a fact of life, particularly in traditional contracts. It is a matter of policy whether to include this as a factor within the fee estimate.

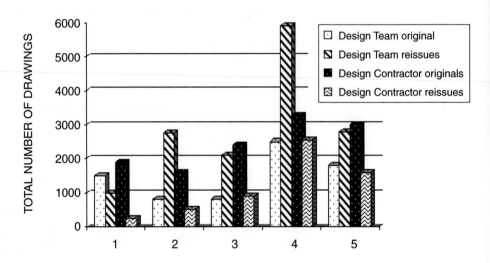

20 Analysis of drawings produced for five large office buildings built between 1998 and 1990. *Source: Gray* et al. *(1994)*

Cost calculation for estimate 'C': preliminary estimate

Total project time

Table 66

Project stage	Time allowance (days)			
	P	A	T	S
A. Inception and B. Feasibility	4.5	6.25	18.5	2
C. Outline proposals	6.75	19.25	63.25	2
D. Scheme design	6.75	25	47.25	4
E. Detail design	4.25	17	45.25	4
F. Production information and G. Bills of quantities	5.25	43.25	191.25	4
H. Tender action	3	11		6
J. Project planning	3	8		2
K. Operations on site	3	37	7	4
L Completion and M. Feedback	2	4	3	2
Employee-specific total	38.5	170.75	375.5	30
Practice total (days)	**615**			
Practice total (hours)	**4,611**			

Cost calculation for estimate: final estimate

Total costs of each employee type involvement in the project

Table 67

Employee type	Total involvement	Cost (£/day) in project (days)	Total (days × £/day)
Partner (P)	38.5	189.41	7,292.28
Architect (A)	170.75	138.85	23,708.63
Technician (T)	375.5	116.10	43,595.55
Secretary (S)	30	105.32	3,159.6
Total cost of employee time to project		**77,756.06**	

Additional factors

Travel expenses: £2,769
Survey fees: £13,200.

Cost calculation – preliminary estimate: results

Therefore,
Total = £77,756,06 + £2,769 + £13,200 = **£93,725.06**
Add an additional 2.5% to account for inflation = **£96,068.19**

Feasibility check percentage time requirements

Table 68

Employee type	Total no. of employee type	Total involvement in project (days)	Working days/year	Percentage of working year required for project per office employee	Total of working year (months) for project per office employee
Partner (P)	2	38.5	228	8.5	1.02
Architect (A)	1	170.75	230	74.2	8.9
Technician (T)	3	375.5	232	54	6.48
Secretary (S)	1	30	232	12.9	1.548

Calculation example: technician:

Involvement per person = total involvement of employee type/total no. of employee type = 375.5/3 = 125.16.
Percentage of working year = (involvement per person/working days per year for employee type) × 100 = (125.16/232) × 100 = **54%**.

Feasibility check: analysis

Analysis of the data in Table 69 clearly shows that a problem exists in the allocation of the work for the project throughout the practice. As already defined, the job would be run by an architect, overseen by the partners, with the majority of the drawing work completed by architectural technologists. However, the three technologists currently employed at the practice would be required to work solidly for 54% of the working year (or 6.48 months) to complete the envisaged workload. As it would be inadvisable to dedicate the entire practice to the completion of one major project, this would cause considerable disruption to the other projects currently being completed at the practice.

Additional resources

Additional resources, both human and physical, may be required to complete the project within a respectable time frame.

Additional human resources: two technical staff: £17,500 × 2 = £35,000
Additional physical resources: two networked computers: £3,000
CAD software: £2,000.

The additional physical resource costs should not be reflected directly in the fee-bid tender for the project but absorbed by the office's budget for expansion.

Revised percentage time requirements

Table 69

Employee type	Total no. of employee type	Total involvement in project (days)	Working days/year	Percentage of working year required for project per office employee	Total of working year (months) for project per office employee
Partner (P)	2	38.5	228	8.5	1.02
Architect (A)	1	170.75	230	74.2	8.9
Technician (T)	5	375.5	232	32.4	3.88
Secretary (S)	1	30	232	12.9	1.548

Revised office running costs for additional staff

Table 70

Revised item	Original total (£) (for seven staff)	Revised total (for nine staff) + 28.5% (£)
Electricity	1,000	1,285
Gas	1,500	1,927.50
Telephone	4,500	5,782.50
Computer consumables	1,200	1,542
Computer equipment	6,000	7,710
CAD training	1,750	2,248.75
Software updates	1,200	1,542
PII	£3 million @ 5,125	£5 million @ 7,000
Office refreshments	600	771
Postage charges	350	449.75
Stationary	2,300	2,955.50
Printing	2,500	3,212.50
Salaries	150,000	185,000
Unaffected items total	38,030	38,030
Totals	**216,055**	**259,456.50**

Therefore:
Total office running cost per year per employee = [total running costs (revised) − total salaries]/productive staff members = (£259,456.50 − £185,000)/9 = **£8,272.94**.

Revised employee-specific cost per day: job specific

Table 71

Employee type 'A'	Assumed salary (£) 'C'	Holiday allowance (days/year) 'D'	Calculation $\dfrac{(C + 8{,}272.94)}{260 - (D - 8)}$	Employee-specific costs (£/day) 'E'
Partner (P)	33,750	24	$\dfrac{33{,}750 + 8{,}272.94}{228}$	184.31 (E1)
Architect (A)	22,500	22	$\dfrac{22{,}500 + 8{,}272.94}{230}$	133.79 (E2)
Technician (T)	17,500	20	$\dfrac{17{,}500 + 8{,}272.94}{232}$	111.09 (E3)
Secretary (S)	15,000	20	$\dfrac{15{,}000 + 8{,}272.94}{232}$	100.31 (E4)

Revised total costs of each employee type involvement in the project

Table 72

Employee type	Total involvement in project (days)	Revised cost (£/day)	Total (days × £/day) (£)
Partner (P)	38.5	184.31	7,095.94
Architect (A)	170.75	133.79	22,844.64
Technician (T)	375.5	111.09	41,714.26
Secretary (S)	30	100.31	3,009.3
Total			**74,664.14**

Cost calculation for final estimate: results

Cost calculation = total cost of employee time to project + travel expenses + survey fee.

Therefore:
Total = £74,664.14 + £2,769 + £13,200 = **£90,933.14**
Add an additional 2.5% for inflation = **£92,898.97**
Labour expenditure for project (**estimate**) = **£92,898.97**.

Precontract programme

The precontract programme is shown in Figure 21.

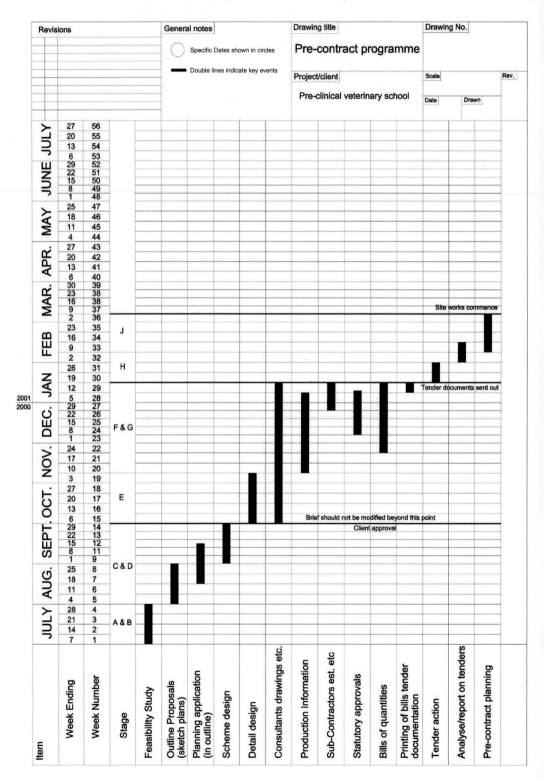

Summary of results

Office costs per man-year (current figures)

Total cost per man-year = **£32,007.80**.

The average costs per man-day (current figures) are shown in Table 73.

Table 73

Employee type 'A'	Assumed salary (£) 'C'	Holiday allowance (days/year) 'D'	Calculation $\dfrac{(C + 9{,}436.4)}{260 - (D - 8)*}$	Employee-specific costs (£/day)
Partner (P)	33,750	24	$\dfrac{33{,}750 + 9{,}436.4}{228}$	189.41 (E1)
Architect (A)	22,500	22	$\dfrac{22{,}500 + 9{,}436.4}{230}$	138.85 (E2)
Technician (T)	17,500	20	$\dfrac{17{,}500 + 9{,}436.4}{232}$	116.10 (E3)
Secretary (S)	15,000	20	$\dfrac{15{,}000 + 9{,}436.4}{232}$	105.32 (E4)

Assuming 260 working days in a year and eight days' Bank Holiday.

Average cost per man-day (revised figures with additional staff)

Table 74

Employee type 'A'	Assumed salary (£) 'C'	Holiday allowance (days/year) 'D'	Calculation $\dfrac{(C + 8{,}272.94)}{260 - (D - 8)*}$	Employee-specific costs (£/day)
Partner (P)	33,750	24	$\dfrac{33{,}750 + 8{,}272.94}{228}$	184.31 (E1)
Architect (A)	22,500	22	$\dfrac{22{,}500 + 8{,}272.94}{230}$	133.79 (E2)
Technician (T)	17,500	20	$\dfrac{17{,}500 + 8{,}272.94}{232}$	111.09 (E3)
Secretary (S)	15,000	20	$\dfrac{15{,}000 + 8{,}272.94}{232}$	100.31 (E4)

The labour expenditure for the project = **£92,898.97**.

21 Precontract programme
(opposite)

D Analysis and conclusions

Introduction

Methodology

Summary of calculations

Analysis of the practice status
*Summary of current practice conditions:
current workload requirements
Analysis of current infrastructure: human
Analysis of infrastructure: physical
Possible 1–5–10-year practice forecast
Factors: STEEP analysis
Practice SWOT (strengths, weakness,
opportunities, threats) analysis
Summary of employee type involvement for
the project
Practice conclusions*

Analysis of the project
*Positive/negative aspects of the job for the
practice*

Analysis of external competition

**Additional factors to convert the
estimate into a fee-bid tender**
*Perceived value of project to AB Architects
Contract strategy
Profit margin
Payment of fees by programmed instalments*

Final summary

Introduction

To convert an analytical estimate into a tender fee bid, several additional factors need to be addressed. The first is undoubtedly whether the practice wishes to pursue the commission. The tendering process itself can be a drain upon the practice's human and financial resources. If it is deemed that the project type, size, location or level of remuneration is incompatible with the practice, then the tendering process should be terminated. It could also be deemed that the fee-bid tender submitted by the practice would simply be uneconomic when compared with the other competing parties.

To explore the compatibility of the project with the practice, it is necessary to analyse further both the current status of the practice and the advantages (in addition to the purely financial aspects) of the project to the practice. This will provide a clear indication of the practice's capability to complete the job and the lengths it will go to to gain the commission.

In addition, other factors such as profit, contract strategy, payment by programmed instalments, etc. will be discussed to complete the process of converting an estimate price into a tender fee for the project.

Methodology

The methodology diagram is shown in Figure 22.

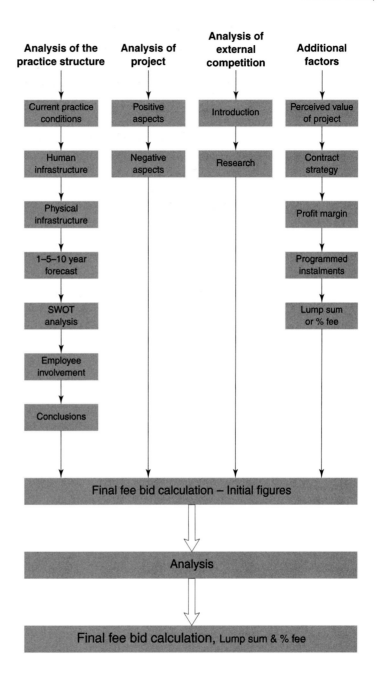

22 Methodology diagram

Summary of calculations

Table 75

(1) Approximation budget figure for the building: £4 million
(2) RIBA indicative fee scales for this building: lump sum £264,843 or 6.75%
(3) Workstage totals (days) (Table 63):

Partners	39 days	
Architect	171 days	
Technologist	375 days	
Total	585 days	
Revised in Table 69	615 days	£77,756
(4) Checking drawings (Table 66)	25 days	£3,160
(5) Transport: car, train, taxi		£2,769
(6) Survey fees		13,200
Subtotal		£96,885
Allow 2.5% for inflation		£2,422
Subtotal (excluding all disbursements, statutory fees, profit, etc.)		£99,307
Add:		
Contingencies (2.5%)	£138,645	
Furniture (2.5%)	£452,938	
Incinerator (2.5%)	£195,010	£19,666
Archaeology (1%)	£19,700	£197
Total		**£119,170** (carried forward)

It has been the philosophy within the analytical estimation section of this exercise to relate probable labour outputs to the number and size of drawings. Although this crude system may pertain as an expedient, it can only remain an approximation. In this illustration, there will probably be a time for conceptualizing the belief and a great deal of abortive work may be invested in the design process. For this reason, particularly bearing in mind that this is a fairly complicated high-specification building, an allowance must be made for this work. Again, this will be a guess, hopefully made from real experience.

Carried forward = £119,170
Say, 4 weeks + 20 days @ £200 for a partner = £4,000
Total labour and overheads = **£123,170**
Add for profit 100% = £123,170
Total analytical fee estimation = **£246,340**

Compared with: indicative fee calculation = £264,843.

Analysis of the practice status

Summary of current practice conditions: current workload requirements

Table 76

Employee type	Number of jobs currently involved with	Expected completion time (working days)
Partner 1	4	–
Partner 1	4	–
Architect	1	100
Architectural technologist 1	2	100
Architectural technologist 2	2	150
Architectural assistant	1	150
Administrative assistant	multiple	–

Analysis of current infrastructure: human

It is assumed that AB Architects is currently employing a minimum number of staff to complete the current practice workload. This method of working provides several operating problems. With such a small team allocated to each project, employee time is critical. Employee absence, planned or unplanned, effectively stops output on that employee's specific job. There is very little scope for covering absenteeism by the internal workforce. This is a problem that AB Architects has identified and may seek to rectify in a number of ways. First, the company can establish links with a number of external freelance workers. This provides the practice with a highly flexible workforce that can be drafted onto a project at a defined stage to cope with additional workloads. These freelance workers may specialize in certain fields, ranging from technical detailing to computer visualization. Freelance workers operate externally and their involvement in a project may be very short-term.

AB Architects may also have established links with employment agencies that specialize in recruitment for the construction industry. Agency staff can be employed to supplement the practice's internal human resources and usually work for about 3–6 months on a particular project.

AB Architects should not, however, be opposed to expansion.

Analysis of infrastructure: physical

AB Architects is clearly in a transitional stage as a practice. It appears to be evolving from being a small firm – an amalgam of two sole practitioners – to a small-/medium-sized practice by regional standards. This provides some defined operational difficulties. In this case, these difficulties may not involve physical spatial requirements as the practice is housed in offices that could accommodate an architects' firm of around 25 architectural staff and administrative assistants. It is assumed that the practice is adequately resourced in computer equipment and associated physical hardware. The problems would arise from a lack of supporting resources, especially for a project outside the practice's traditional project sphere. The company may lack the technical literature, product library and specialized IT resources that enable employees to access information quickly and concisely. This would decrease the efficiency of employees and reduce the flexibility of the practice to attempt specialized projects. However, it is determined to win this project.

Possible 1–5–10-year practice forecast

Table 77

Years in advance	Practice size (number of employees)	Practice size (average contract value, £ millions) excluding inflation	Dominant project type	General project location
1	7	1.2	residential	regional
5	10	2.0	residential, educational	regional
10	12	2.5	residential, commercial	regional

Factors: STEEP analysis

The factors that may have an effect on the running of the practice and this market fall mainly into five categories:

Social:
- Staff membership of sports' clubs: social membership identifying potential clients, networking, etc.
- Population shifts
- Urban regeneration
- Poverty gap
- Popularity of green issues.

Technical:
- CPD requirement by RIBA
- Computer advances: obsolete equipment
- Construction product advances/failures
- Energy efficiency.

Economic:
- Interest and mortgage rate changes
- Regional development/investment
- Grant systems' altering
- Lottery
- Poverty gap.

Environmental:
- Urban regeneration
- Change in the character of the office location/office image
- Ecological issues.

Political:
- Change of government/planning law
- RIBA political activity
- Sustainable development/transport policy
- Energy policy
- Funding
- CDM regulations
- Council housing/housing associations.

Such 'big issues' may have a bearing on this or any job. When considering the strategic development of a practice, it is wise to think the unthinkable and prepare for the unimaginable.

Practice SWOT (strengths, weakness, opportunities, threats) analysis

Table 78

Strengths	Weakness	Opportunities	Threats
Compact structure	Human resources	Internal resourcing	Specialized in a singular project type
Experience in the chosen project type	Lack of support resources	Project diversification	Internal resources
Multidisciplinary approach	Internal communication	Project location expansion	Lack of a critical mass in resources
IT platform	Regional outlook		
Physical resources			
Practice location			

Summary of employee type involvement for the project

Table 79

Employee type	Total number of employee type	Total involvement in project (days)	Percentage of working year required for the project per office employee	Total of working year (months) for the project per office employee
Partner (P)	2	38.5	8.5	1.02
Architect (A)	1	170.75	74.2	8.9
Technician (T)	5	375.5	32.4	3.88
Secretary (S)	1	30	12.9	1.548

From Section C: Revised percentage time requirements.

Practice conclusions

In Figure 16 (see page 84), it was already defined that to run the job on a traditional form of contract, AB Architects' extant human resources would be insufficient. As specified in Table 74 (see page 117), additional staff members could be employed to cope with the additional workload. These staff members could be on a year's provisional contract so that the practice would retain an element of flexibility if economic conditions and/or workloads varied. The investment in additional IT if required is not the major factor that it once was, and thus could be easily accommodated on such a small scale into the office budget.

For the sake of completing the calculations, two additional technical staff were employed to complete the job. There are, however, other methods to cope with a major addition to the office workload. As described above, freelance workers and agency staff could provide the additional human resources to complete the practice's project involvement.

Internal reallocation of the workload is a form of management strategy that could implement a framework to cope with the additional workload. For the calculations in Table 79, a traditional framework for an architect-led internal project team overseen by a partner and supported by technical staff was envisaged. Moving the emphasis away from an architect and towards a partner would increase the internal costs of the job, but it would unlock a large amount of the architect's time which could be dedicated to running the drawings' aspect of the job within the office. Careful calculations of this method would be required to assess its viability.

To cope with the required workload of the job, AB Architects could employ a local site agent to act as a first point of contact for the contractor. This person's involvement in the project could vary from a permanent site agent located on-site with IT links to the practice to a more casual approach of a local site agent who could visit the site as required, to a minimum of once a week. Careful consideration of this person's project involvement, defined role and cost implication would need to be conducted and programmed into the total office cost for completing the project.

Care would also be required to ascertain whether the project was of such a size and potential to merit the forging of professional links with a locally based architectural practice. Many small practices have taken on jobs beyond their previous capacity, only to discover that the job was withdrawn by the client and investments in new resources caused serious hardship – even bankruptcy. To join with a larger practice may bolster financial and resource instabilities. Again, a smaller practice's involvement and role would need to be carefully calculated. In general, it is felt that although the project is outside the practice's normal project sphere, location and size, several management strategies could be implemented to provide an internal framework sufficiently resourced to complete the project.

Analysis of the project

Positive/negative aspects of the job for the practice

Table 80

Positive	Negative
Increasing the practice's area of expertise and portfolio	Project will occupy a large amount of practice time. If problems arise, this can seriously affect yearly profit margins
Highlighting the practice in a new area	Outside of the practice's traditional project sphere
Links to a major university, with possible additional projects	
Guaranteed office workload for the project's duration	
Possible national exposure through architectural periodicals	

Analysis of external competition

The ability to convert an estimate of costs for the proposed work into a commercial tender needs careful judgement, coupled with an assessment of the odds. It must ultimately be a gamble, although the competent architectural manager will reduce the odds as much as possible by prudent analysis of the facts.

First, one should look internally at the current and projected workload of the office. It may not be a question of 'do we want this job?' but rather 'do we need this job?' 'Are our present staff working to full capacity, and is there sufficient work in the pipeline to sustain a healthy period of practice?' In which case, this tender can be more relaxed and a good profit should be the objective (Figure 23).

Alternatively, work in the office may be short-lived and the management's decisions may be a balance between reducing staff members and putting in a keen (less profit) bid. There is a saying: 'The more hungry is the hunter, the more accurate is his arrow.' The possibility of a serious fall in the workload will heighten the awareness of both internal inefficiencies and external completion.

Symes *et al.* (1995), in discussing architects' fees, wrote:

Clients are not so likely to follow simple appointment procedures such as taking soundings and choosing an architect on the basis of trusted advice. They are now more likely to run a complex selection process comparing a range of possible design teams. Fee bids have become an important feature, which did not exist before, and can now take 10 to 20% of a senior staff member's time. The relationship between client and architect is far less one of gentlemanly trust than it used to be, and one informant commented that as soon as you are no longer treated as a gentleman to be trusted, you cease to behave like one!

Respect from potential clients will, however, be engendered by a commercial approach to fee bidding based on scientific principles. When considering a tender, all influences should be calculated, even in the most subjective of issues. For example, Table 81 attempts to highlight issues that can have a bearing on an

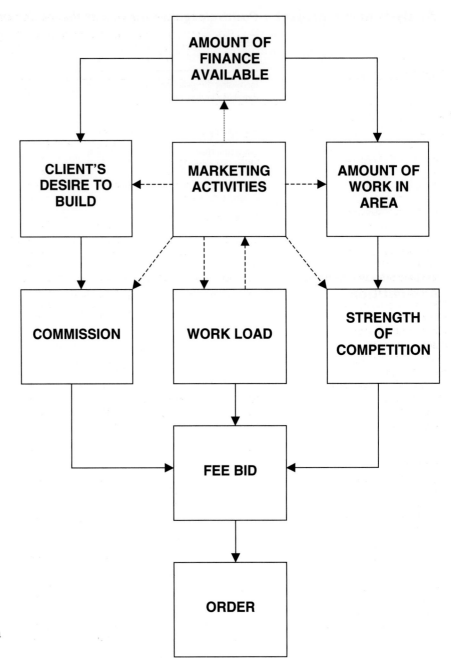

23 External influences on a
fee bid

answer to the question 'Do we want this job?' Questions such as these are a form of risk management. There may be other issues that are firm- or job-specific, but the principle is always the same.

Table 81

	Negative factors			Plus factors		
Self-assessment: the firm						
Experience of the job type	–	–	none	low	moderate	high
Staff experience	–	–	none	low	moderate	high
Specialist skills required	many	some	none	none	–	–
Extra staff	many	some	none	none	–	–
Extra office space	many	some	none	none	–	–
Extra equipment	–	many	some	none	–	–
Assessment of the client						
Client's experience	–	–	none	low	moderate	high
Client's brief	–	–	poor	moderate	reasonable	good
Client's attitude/chemistry	–	disaster	poor	moderate	reasonable	good
Client's reputation	–	disaster	poor	moderate	reasonable	good
Client's expectations	–	–	none	low	average	high
Client's time pressures	–	high	medium	low	nil	–
Client's changes/variations	–	high	average	some	nil	–
Client's programme flexibility	–	–	none	some	moderate	high
Client's cost flexibility	–	–	none	some	moderate	high
Assessment of the project						
Degree of complexity	complex	average	simple	none	–	–
Size and scope	mega	very large	big	normal	–	–
Elements of standardization	–	–	none	some	average	high
Planning difficulties	high	average	few	none	–	–
Legal obstacles	high	average	few	none	–	–
Budget adequacy	–	–	poor	good	–	–
Time allowance	–	–	poor	good	–	–
End-user conflicts	high	average	few	none	–	–
Consultant report						
Reputation experience	–	–	poor	some	moderate	high
Availability	–	difficult	poor	good	excellent	–
Skill/compatibility	–	none	poor	some	moderate	high
Chemistry with the architects	–	none	poor	some	moderate	high
Coordination skills	–	none	poor	some	moderate	high
Contact with the client						
Degree of responsibilities	–	architect biased	shared	shared	client biased	–
Future PI insurability	–	–	poor	good	–	–
Vicarious liabilities	–	–	poor	good	–	–
Collateral warranties	–	–	poor	good	–	–
Other performance demands	–	–	poor	good	–	–
Supervision of the works	complete	moderate	some	none	–	–
Employment of a clerk of works	–	–	no	yes	–	–
Fees/compensation						
Funding/cash flow	–	difficult	poor	occasional	good	–
Client's ability to pay	–	–	low	high	–	–
Cost of doing the work	–	–	high	low	–	–
Profit expectancy	–	–	low	medium	high	–
Limitation of duties	–	–	low	some	medium	high
Future claims risk	high	some	low	nil	–	–
Warranties/assessments	–	many	some	nil	–	–
Types of construction						

Table 81 cont.

	Negative factors			Plus factors		
Traditional	–	some	none	100%	–	–
New/experimental	all	some	few	none	–	–
New materials	all	some	few	none	–	–
Foundations	–	complex	poor	good	–	–
Exposure/weather	–	coastal	exposed	sheltered	–	–
Maintenance considerations	high	many	few	none	–	–
Market trends						
Is this a 'real' prestige job?	–	no	maybe	yes	good	–
Will other work follow?	–	no	maybe	some	moderate	high
Will work increase skills?	–	–	no	some	many	–
Is the firm being 'used?'	–	–	yes	no	–	–
Is the market increasing?	–	–	no	yes	–	–
Other factors						
–						
–						
–						
	C	B	A	D	E	F

Add up the ticks in columns A–F, multiply columns B and E by 5, multiply columns C and F by 10, total A – C and D – F, take the smaller number from the larger number = risk quotient ±.

Additional factors to convert the estimate into a fee-bid tender

Perceived value of project to AB Architects

As argued above, in the advantages of the project for AB architects, this project would have several positive implications for the practice apart from monetary value, and as a result, the firm would be submitting a competitive fee-bid tender for the project.

Contract strategy

It is often the case that the client already has a clear idea of what form of contract strategy to pursue. In such cases, the fee-bid tender would be exclusively tailored for this approach. No such information is provided in this instance and, therefore, a contract strategy that best fits AB Architects' criteria can be pursued. For a practice of AB Architects' size and resources, the contract strategy is of key importance to the estimation of a fee-bid tender. Although a traditional form of contract has been assumed for the calculations required for Sections A–C, to ignore the possible options would be over simplistic.

The design-and-build (D&B) option is a type of contract strategy that AB Architects increasingly promotes. In this case study, a novated form of D&B contract strategy would ideally suit a practice of AB Architects' size. A novated form of D&B contract allows the client to appoint an architect who oversees the project to the tendering stage. The architect then is novated for the rest of the contract, working with the appointed main contractor to the completion of the contract. The main advantage to AB Architects with such a form of contract is that the involvement on the job with the practice is reduced. Thus, a practice of AB Architects' size can complete larger contracts than it could under a more traditional contract strategy. However, owing to this reduction in project involvement, the fees the practice could command for the project would be significantly less. A rough rule of thumb is that D&B fees for a project are roughly half those that could be expected under a traditional contract strategy.

Profit margin

If commissioned, the project would form the basis of the practice's work for the next 24 months. As a result, although the practice is keen to submit a competitive tender price, there must be in an element of profit programmed. Some architects' general practice policy on profit is to submit a cost + 100% estimate where office labour expenses can be accurately quantified.

Payment of fees by programmed instalments

Receiving regular and substantial fees from projects is vital to maintain cash flow within the practice. Fee payment based upon completed workstages provides a framework for payment based upon defined stages in the building contract. Such a fee-instalment programme can also provide scope for increasing the competitiveness of the fee-bid tender. By promoting a system of forward-weighting fees for a project, an architect can actively reduce the total fee bid but compensate this loss by receiving a greater majority of the fees during the contract's preliminary workstages. This front-loading can create difficulties if, for example, the extent of the site supervision is greatly extended (see Figure 26, page 138).

Final summary

Estimate of building cost – including site works, etc.:
Estimate based on RIBA indicative scales = £264.843 or 6.62%
Estimate (analytical approach) = £246,340 or 6.16%

Tender – may be up to £300,000 depending on the factors considered elsewhere and subject to the decision by the partners. On the other hand, a difference of 0.46% between the two methods may encourage the directors/partners to offer a fee bid nearer to £246,000.

To arrive at the final bid, the average of the estimates may be adopted and it is subjected to circumstances as evaluated in Table 82 and expressed as a percentage.

Table 82

Concern		Effect on bid	Weighting
Explorative works: unknown issues	possible	higher	+5
Bias effect of high cost fit-out/services	significant	lower	−20
Omissions in estimate C	probable	higher	+15
Desirability of the project	high	lower	−2
Competition from other bids	low (lots of work around)	higher	+2
Current workload	medium (but need to secure future projects)	lower	−2
Familiarity with the project type	new project type	higher	+4
Familiarity with the client	none	higher	+2
Proximity of the site to the practice	regional (40 miles)	lower	−4
		Total	0% change

For Workstages A and B, the fees are charged on a time basis (Table 83), which have been adjusted to suit the complexity of the building type.

Table 83

	£/hour	RIBA Journal survey	Chappell and Willis (2000)
Partner	£140	£75	£130
Associate	£120	£65	£100
Architect	£75	£46	£70
Part III Student	£45	£40	–
Technician	£50	£45	–

Note that there is a wide variation between the amounts quoted in the professional architectural press. Monitor Press, in a newsletter to lawyers, suggested that partners (involved in commercial liquidation) routinely aspire to charge their clients £400 or more per hour.

Part III The tender trap

The worked example has been taken from the point where the client's brief has been established and a sketch scheme approved. Everybody (especially the client) at that stage will need to confirm a budget price for the building before any further action is taken. The client will need, in all probability, to raise funds and obtain

New Build

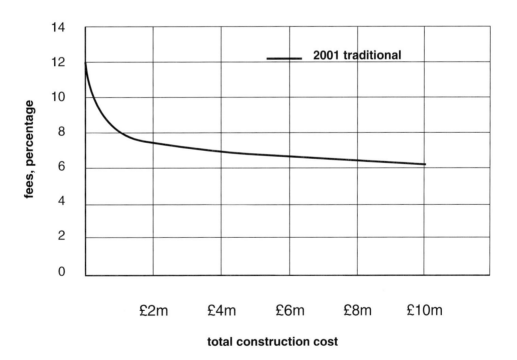

24 New build. *Source: Architects fees, Mirza & Nacey Research (2001)*

all approvals before proceeding; the architect will need to know the financial constraints that will be imposed on the design.

In this illustration, a comparison has been made between the figures provided by a professional quantity surveyor and standard price books on a price based on floor areas (measured between external walls and over internal walls). The resultant figure was rounded to a £4 million construction contract.

With this essential information, the architect can, if he or she chooses, take the easy route and refer to the RIBA's indicative percentage fee scales for normal services (Figures 14 and 15). In this example, there is both new build and conversion works, so figures from both have been used (Mirza & Nacey Research (2001), Figures 24 and 25). Within the construction industry and design professions, it is accepted that architectural fees for design and build work is generally 3 to 4% lower than for traditional working methods. As a guide, reference was also made to Spon's similar charts and the results did not show any dramatic differences. The advantage of taking the *ad valorem* route is obviously speed (it takes only a few minutes to make the calculation). On the other hand, the architect is in possession of a final figure only, with no knowledge of any control budgets. For example, a myth has developed within the architectural profession that the standard (new indicative) fees could be divided into three equal parts: labour, overheads and profit. Competition has now made firms look far more closely at their accountancy and costing systems so that controls in expenditure can be built into the management process as the work proceeds.

Refurbishment

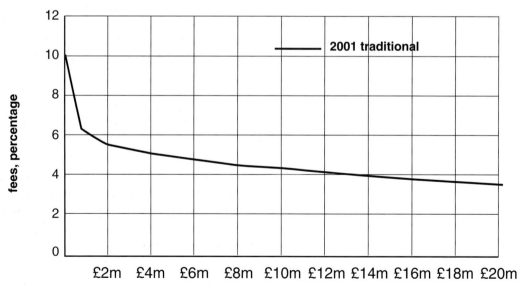

25 Refurbishment. *Source: Architects fees, Mirza & Nacey Research (2001)*

This case study has shown that a detailed (although time-consuming) method can be employed in the preparation of the fee bid, which will provide figures for planning the design process as well as budgets of expenditure. The first analysis necessary is to look at the firm's financial accounts for one (or more) years and analyse the figures into identifiable areas. It is from this analysis that the true cost of the practice can be identified together with the net cost of each productive member of staff.

Unless the cost profile of the firm changes dramatically (perhaps the senior partner arrives at the office with another new car), then the analysis for the purpose of calculating fees needs to be done only once every year and reference be made to it for each bid. At this point, the cost of all overheads and staff costs will be to hand. It is then necessary to project this information to the proposed fee calculation with the big unknown factor being the time that each person will take to produce an exciting building, accurately within the client's brief, and to the desired quality and time scale. The fee estimator at this stage will break down the work into small areas and build up a picture of time allocations.

The system chosen for this exercise was, first, to produce a probable schedule of drawings that might be necessary for this job. Against each drawing is set an estimated time for partner, architect and technologist. The total labour and associated overhead costs are produced and a figure is assessed for profit.

A simplified method (although less accurate) may be used by just multiplying the estimated number of drawings by a factor for labour and adding the site supervision time. For example, if there are 100 drawings, each of which can be produced in three working days, and site supervision is twenty days, then:

$$(100 \text{ drawings} \times 3 \text{ man-days}) + 20 \text{ days} = 320 \text{ man-days}.$$

Multiplying 320 man-days by the average cost of each technical person gives a net cost potential before profit and other factors are taken into consideration. Then the decision has to be made about how much the fee bid will be to achieve the commission and to show a profit.

Stage payments

It is usual in the tender bid to give the client some indication of his or her financial commitments over time. The work may be paid on a monthly basis of equal payments or, more frequently, a formula is agreed at the tender stage. The work is divided into workstages as according to the RIBA *Plan of Work*, although as Chappell and Willis (2000) suggest, 'It is not always easy to pinpoint activities within a particular stage, because the whole process is continuous and some activities can be accommodated in several stages.' However, this does provide a useful profession-wide basis for interim payments (Figure 26)

In RIBA's *Risk Management for Architects* (Pepperell and Cecil c.1990), architects are extolled to 'formulate commissions and fee agreements with meticulous care, ensuring that the firm has the resources and competence which a commission requires is not only sound common sense but a requirement of the Code of Professional Conduct'. The document further recommends the following 'watch points':

Work Stage		Proportion of Fee%
A	Appraisal	(usually charged
B	Strategic brief	on a time basis)
C	Outline Proposals	20
D	Detailed Proposals	20
E	Final Proposals	15
F	Production Information	20
G	Tender Documentation	2
H	Tender Action	1
J	Mobilization	1
K	Construction to Practical Completion	20
L	After Practical Completion	1
		100%

26 Proportion of the fee by work stage. *Source: RIBA (1999c)*

- Always aim to base your appointment on the conditions set out in *Architect's Appointment*. (State the version used and its date of publication).
- Ensure that arrangements for payment do not expose you to extending greater credit than you can afford.
- Render accounts regularly and take action if they are not honoured.
- Keep good records, so that you know what a job actually costs you. They will be invaluable for future fee quotations.
- If you quote a lump sum fee based on the assumed total project cost, include a provision for adjusting the fee if costs increase.
- Beware of quoting 'all-inclusive' fees. Make clear the difference between disbursements and expenses. Party wall agreements, rights of light, surveys, etc. can be unexpectedly costly.
- Never allow payment of your fees to be conditional upon obtaining planning permission or other matters over which you have no control.

Risk management

Risk is a function of both the probability of an adverse event occurring and its impact. The impact may manifest itself generally as any combination of:

- financial loss;
- time delay;
- performance loss; and
- status and confidence.

In some ways, the loss of status and confidence may prove the greatest loss. For instance, any loss of confidence by clients will dramatically reduce the size of the order book. Similarly, any loss of confidence on the part of a bank manager may result in loans being recalled and performance loss leading to financial ruin.

Whilst risk is usually an abstract concept referred to in subjective terms, one should have a notion of the degree or quantification of probability:

- H = high probability: more likely to happen than not – more than 50%
- M = medium probability: fairly likely to happen – 20–30%
- L = low probability: less likely to happen – less than 20%.

Reducing risk exposure means paying attention to detail in a number of areas, bearing in mind that any risk avoidance measure must, of course, be legal to be effective. Risk avoidance should also fall within the realms of reasonable professional codes of practice.

Risk management should be part of the overall planning and operation of the practice. Defining a practice's goals and objectives enables the risk to be identified as well as the time scale involved. This process calls for a strategic plan that allows for regular reviews of progress and standards, as well as financial monitoring and forecasting. In this way, one can identify any unintended deviations. A well-run practice makes for good risk management.

Before managing the risk, it needs to be properly identified. Look at those work practices that increase risk and those most likely to reduce it. The following headings make a practical starting point:

- Client-briefing procedure
- Good management practices
- Effective communications
- Known claims' risk areas
- Client selection
- Professional liability under the law
- Collateral warranties
- Protection via indemnity insurance
- Protection via quality assurance.

It is vital to have either a contract or a letter to prove the basis of the contract at the outset of every commission. The scope and limits of each commission must be properly defined and must include the terms upon which one has agreed to work and a definition of the services one has agreed to provide (use the RIBA's Architect's Appointment Causes as reference points). Also, take into account the following risk controls.

Warn the client about any services that will be needed but which you do not intend to provide. For example, supervision is the traditional duty of the contractor or others and should be one of your excluded services.

If attendance is to be provided with inspection or observation duties, define what is meant by these terms and clarify the degree to which involvement is intended. Do not agree to any extra duties without an appropriate written agreement of limitation and an extra fee to cover the risk.

Make it clear that all work has to be designed on the basis that, where appropriate, it will require and receive proper and regular maintenance. This work is to be in accordance with good trade practice and manufacturers' instructions. If the client insists on using materials, components or systems that would not normally be recommended, disclaim liability in writing for any failure before they are put into use and say these would not be your choice.

Agree clearly the basis on which you will be paid. This may mean stipulating advance payments for the job setting-up cost and that interest will be charged on overdue accounts at 5% above the prevailing bank rate.

Make sure the client understands what he or she is getting for his or her money. If the client does not want to pay for a full service, disclaim in writing any personal liability for any latent defect resulting from a partial service. A clear brief at the outset can save many problems later.

Understand the professional contracts, as well as those used by the client, for the project. Ensure that the firm is not accepting liabilities that exceed those owed by you or required under statute. Remember, too, to try to limit the exposure in terms of time. For example, in a contract signed under seal, the basic contract liability period is twelve years instead of the six years applying to contracts signed under hand.

As a summary of check listings that require caution in risk management generally and fee bidding in particular, see Sawczuk (1996). The consultant terms of appointment requiring caution are shown in Table 84.

Table 84

Agreement to agree: should not be used as the future agreement is not defined

As built and record drawings: there is a distinct difference between these terms. It is more usual to provide record drawings

Collateral warranty: check the working and conditions of the collateral warranty with your professional indemnity insurers and solicitors. Try to use standard formats previously agreed by your advisers

Delegated design: note that the employer will often not permit you to delegate design. Therefore, if there is a specialist design input required, bring this to the employer's attention and obtain their permission. In addition, ask that the employer appoints the specialist direct, thereby making sure you are not responsible for design by others

Ensure: unless totally within your power, do not ensure to do anything

Feasibility and viability: there is a distinct difference between these tasks. The consultant should confine the appointment to his or her own specialist skills. For example, the architect may be able to prepare plans to show that it is feasible to build a factory on a certain site, but it is unlikely that he or she would have the skills to prove it is viable

Fitness for purpose: avoid this phrase. Insurers probably will not give you cover

Highly professional standard: do not promote yourself as much better than your professional peers. If you do, you will be judged accordingly, which increases your risk

Innovation: if you are embarking into an area of unknown risk, obtain the client's approval and their acceptance of the increased risk

Liability: your professional indemnity insurers will not cover liability greater than that under the common law of tort

Partial service: define absolutely what is and what is not in your duties. Do not accept responsibility for other duties not within your control

Specialist work: some specialist work is beyond the consultant's expertise to design and, therefore, the consultant must advise the employer to engage an appropriate consultant direct

Supervision and inspection: in most agreements, the consultant will be making periodic inspections and not be supervising the works. The employer must be made aware of the difference and given the option of employing resident staff. Strike out supervision from the agreement if it is not being provided

To the satisfaction of: this is not easily definable and it is better to provide a service to certain defined standards, such as British Standards, or offer to provide reasonable skill and care

Warranties and guarantees: do not give a warranty or guarantee for the performance of the contractor, other parties to the contract, the performance of building materials or anything else beyond your control

---

Risk-management assessment meetings should be held at frequent intervals by all teams working on a project. In some cases, for example when ISO-9001 certification procedures are in place, risk- and quality-management systems become part of standard office protocol.

Variations and changes by the client are an unfortunate feature of the modern construction scene. Clients should be advised that any changes cost increasingly more as the work proceeds. For example, to move the position of a door during the design stage means only a minor change to a drawing and at minimal cost, whilst if the door had to be moved after it had been installed into the building, the situation would be quite different (Figure 27).

Keeping all variations to the early part of the design process has the effect of saving money; later decisions incur costs.

The potential for saving money at the design stage is far greater than during the building and maintenance stages (Figures 28 and 29).

Similarly, resources in the form of man-hours in design can be greatly reduced by having full input by clients and by manufacturers and contractors at the earliest possible moment. Austin Williams (2001), in discussing a project called COGENT that studied performance in construction, noted that the typical number of man-hours could be saved by making early decisions and by involving all parties (including contractors) at the concept stage. It was shown that a possible saving of 100% of man-hours could be achieved (Figure 30). In other words, there was a possible saving of 50% in designers' time due to taking a 'right first time' attitude over the more conventional iterative design process.

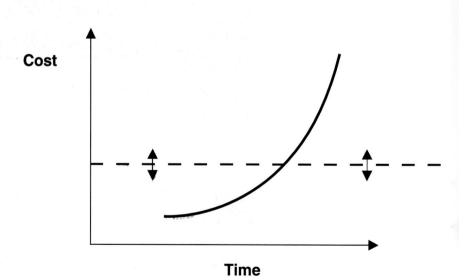

27 Effects of cost variations over time

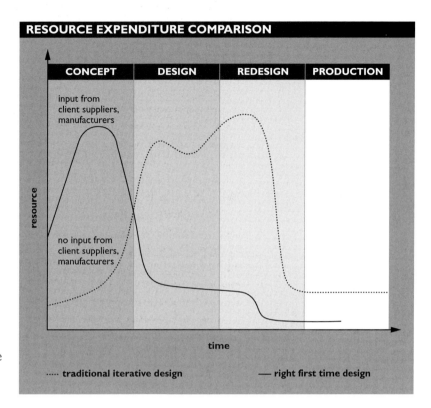

28 Effects of the early involvement of specialists in the design process on resource expenditure

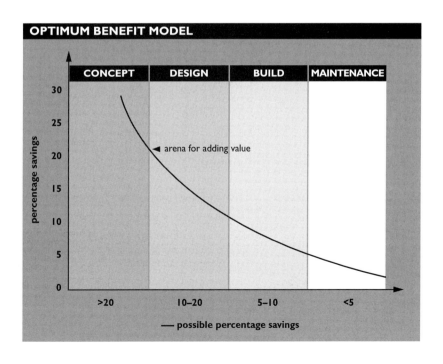

29 Optimum benefit model.
Source: Williams (2001)

TYPICAL MAN-HOURS EXPENDED		
STAGE	**CONVENTIONAL**	**CONSTRUCTION COGENT**
Concept	10,000	20,000
Design	20,000	7,000
Redesign	30,000	3,000
TOTAL	60,000	30,000

30 Typical man-hours expended. *Source: Williams (2001)*

A final caution

In the event that issues develop from which a dispute begins to emerge, all those involved in a project must exercise caution. For example, one must be aware of the dangers of unguarded e-mails. E-mails are often written casually, but they are disclosable to the other party and a court of law in the event of a dispute. Great care must be taken that no e-mails are distributed that can be used against that individual's company and which give the other side 'ammunition'. Even if embarrassing e-mails are deleted, they are likely to have been disseminated more widely and, in any event, can be recovered from that person's hard drive.

Care must also be taken in relation to 'off the record' or 'without prejudice' discussions or correspondence. Whilst the intention is that such communication would not be revealed to a court, the information given to another party during a dispute can still be put to the other side's strategic use. If a party wants to maintain 'privilege' in a document such that it will not be revealed to the other party in court proceedings, then such documents should be routed through lawyers. Employees must also be informed that they should not destroy documents. If there is a dispute, then all documents must be disclosed, including those prejudicial to one's own case or those that support the other side's case.

Those involved in projects, therefore, must monitor how the implementation is going while addressing and minimizing the risks against the backdrop of the contractual rights and obligations, which should be clearly defined or at least clarified as the project progresses. In other words, any practice must develop a professional culture so that all drawings and communications – even e-mails – can be scrutinized by legal professionals if need be.

Procurement routes affect fees

The choice of procurement route can also be a serious factor when redeeming fees from the 'traditional' route. Figure 31 shows that the average fees charged by consultants in a recent research project were 10.33% for traditional procurement methods against 5.37% for design and build – a saving of 4.96% or almost half.

The worked example has been based on the traditional lump sum building contract and the 'normal' services that an architect has to perform. However, a survey by the BCIS (2001) into the comparison of consultants' fees charged produced the graph shown in Figure 31. This indicates that there are large differences

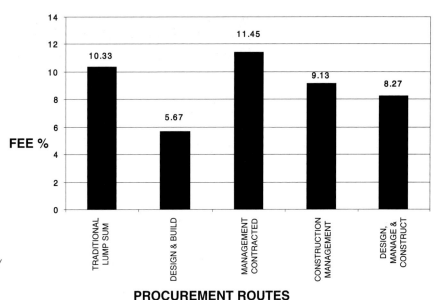

31 Average consultant fee by procurement route. *Source: BCIS (2001)*

in the fees charged between different procurement routes – the lowest being for design and build, and traditional being the second highest to management contracting.

The relative differences between traditional and design and build were confirmed in the *RIBA Journal* (Richardson 2001). These figures, based on the Mirza & Nacey Research (2001) Fees Report, suggest that firms are charging approximately 1.3% less on a £4 million new building for traditional than design and build. Successful fee bidding can only ever be part of the procurement process, part of a professional service. Increasingly, clients are demanding added value where the quality of design and service rank equally as important as price.

Richard Saxon (2000), Chairman of BDP, was quoted as saying that

> Architects, if they are astute, will add their 'brand value' to the team and will emphasise their sales as value enactors, retaining their direct dialogue with clients and users from within the supply team and acting as design team leader alongside the contractor as project leader.

Value for money

According to US Think-Tank Director Ron Baker, hourly billing (and fee bidding) is a big mistake. In a talk to the Managing Partners Forum in October 2001 called 'Trashing the Timesheet', Baker advocated something called 'value pricing', a 'totally new approach to billing', in which professionals charge on the basis of the value to their clients – by results, not by effort. One might ask, 'What is the value of a church to its members?' or 'What is the value of a factory to its owners? or, perhaps, 'What is the value of the Eden Project to its investors?'

Appendix

Architects

DRAWING REGISTER & ISSUE

JOB NO:	SHEET:
001	1

PROJECT:

WE ENCLOSE COPIES OF THE DRAWINGS LISTED BELOW

	DAY			REVISION									
	MONTH												
	YEAR												
DRAWING TITLE	**Drawing No.**	**Scale**	**Size**										
As exist. Site Plan/location plan	001/100	Varies	A1										
As exist. GF plan	001/101	1:100	A1										
As exist. FF plan	001/102	1:100	A1										
As exist. SF plan	001/103	1:100	A1										
As exist. Elevation A	001/104	1:100	A1										
As exist. Elevation B	001/105	1:100	A1										
As exist. Elevation C	001/106	1:100	A1										
As exist. Elevation D	001/107	1:100	A1										
As exist. Section A-A	001/108	1:100	A1										
As exist. Section B-B	001/109	1:100	A1										
As exist. Section C-C	001/110	1:100	A1										
As exist. section D-D	001/111	1:100	A1										

DISTRIBUTION		**NUMBER OF COPIES**							
	Client								
	Main. Contra.								
	Sub-Contractor								
	Sub-Contractor								
	Q.S								

32 Drawing Register & Issue,
Sheet 1

DRAWING REGISTER & ISSUE

PROJECT:		I

JOB NO:	SHEET:
001	**2**

WE ENCLOSE COPIES OF THE DRAWINGS LISTED BELOW

	DAY												
	MONTH												
	YEAR												
DRAWING TITLE	**Drawing No.**	**Scale**	**Size**	**REVISION**									
As prop. Site plan/location plan	001/201	Varies	A1										
As prop. GF plan	001/202	1:100	A1										
As prop. FF plan	001/203	1:100	A1										
As prop. SF plan	001/204	1:100	A1										
As prop. Roof plan	001/205	1:100	A1										
As prop. Elevation A	001/206	1:100	A1										
As prop. Elevation B	001/207	1:100	A1										
As prop. Elevation C	001/208	1:100	A1										
As prop. Elevation D	001/209	1:100	A1										
As prop. Elevation E	001/210	1:100	A1										
As prop. Elevation F	001/211	1:100	A1										
As prop. Elevation G	001/212	1:100	A1										
As prop. Elevation H	001/213	1:100	A1										
As prop. Section A-A	001/214	1:100	A1										
As prop. Section B-B	001/215	1:100	A1										
As prop. Section C-C	001/216	1:100	A1										
As prop. Section D-D	001/217	1:100	A1										
As prop. Elevations A & B	001/218	Nts	A1										
As prop. Elevations C & D	001/219	Nts	A1										
3D models views 1	001/220	Nts	A1										
3D models views 2	001/221	Nts	A1										
Landscaping scheme	001/222	1:500	A1										
Ext. finishes Board 1	001/223	Nts	A2										
Ext. finishes Board 2	001/224	Nts	A2										
DISTRIBUTION				**NUMBER OF COPIES**									
		Client											
		Main. Contra.											
		Sub-Contractor											
		Sub-Contractor											
		Q.S											

33 Drawing Register & Issue,
Sheet 2

Architects

DRAWING REGISTER & ISSUE

PROJECT:	
JOB NO: 001	**SHEET:** 3

WE ENCLOSE COPIES OF THE DRAWINGS LISTED BELOW

				DAY									
				MONTH									
				YEAR									
DRAWING TITLE	Drawing No.	Scale	Size	**REVISION**									
Foundation plan	001/225	1:100	A1										
Fire strategy plan	001/226	1:200	A0										
Ventilation strategy plan	001/227	1:200	A0										
Heating plan	001/228	1:200	A0										
Drainage plan	001/229	1:200	A0										
Ceiling grid layout	001/230	1:200	A0										
Electrical layout plan	001/231	1:200	A0										
Disabled access strategy	001/232	1:200	A1										

DISTRIBUTION		**NUMBER OF COPIES**	
	Client		
	Main. Contra.		
	Sub-Contractor		
	Sub-Contractor		
	Q.S		

34 Drawing Register & Issue,
Sheet 3

Architects

DRAWING REGISTER & ISSUE

PROJECT:

JOB NO:	SHEET:
001	**4**

WE ENCLOSE COPIES OF THE DRAWINGS LISTED BELOW

DAY
MONTH
YEAR

DRAWING TITLE	Drawing No.	Scale	Size	REVISION
Rooms AH1-AH5 typical arrang.	001/233	1:50	A1	
Rooms E1-E14 typical arrang.	001/234	1:50	A1	
Rooms R1-R3 typical arrang.	001/235	1:50	A1	
Rooms LA1-LA3 typical arrang.	001/236	1:50	A1	
Rooms L1-L10 typical arrang.	001/237	1:50	A1	
Rooms T1-T10 typical arrang.	001/238	1:50	A1	
Rooms SS1-SS15 typical arrang.	001/239	1:50	A1	
Rooms C1 & C2 typical arrang.	001/240	1:50	A1	
Rooms AC1-AC16 typical arrang.	001/241	1:50	A1	
Rooms LIB1 typical arrang.	001/242	1:50	A1	
Rooms CR1 & CR2 typical arrang.	001/243	1:50	A1	
Rooms K1 typical arrang.	001/244	1:50	A1	
Rooms AD1-AD4 typical arrang.	001/245	1:50	A1	
Rooms Te1 & Te2 typical arrang.	001/246	1:50	A1	
Rooms ST1 typical arrang.	001/247	1:50	A1	
Rooms WC1-WC6 typical arrang.	001/248	1:50	A1	
Rooms S1-S20 typical arrang.	001/249	1:50	A1	
Rooms P1-P4 typical arrang.	001/250	1:50	A1	

DISTRIBUTION		NUMBER OF COPIES
	Client	
	Main. Contra.	
	Sub-Contractor	
	Sub-Contractor	
	Q.S	

Architects

DRAWING REGISTER & ISSUE

JOB NO:	SHEET:
001	**5**

PROJECT:

WE ENCLOSE COPIES OF THE DRAWINGS LISTED BELOW

	DAY			REVISION
	MONTH			
	YEAR			

DRAWING TITLE	Drawing No.	Scale	Size	REVISION
Detail sheet A: Foundations	001/251	1:5,1:10	A1	
Detail sheet B: Ext. Walls	001/252	1:5,1:10	A1	
Detail sheet C: Int. walls	001/253	1:5,1:10	A1	
Detail sheet D: Windows	001/254	1:5,1:10	A1	
Detail sheet E: Doors	001/255	1:5,1:10	A1	
Detail sheet F: Roof	001/256	1:5,1:10	A1	
Detail sheet G: Stairs	001/257	1:5,1:10	A1	
Detail sheet H: Lifts	001/258	1:5,1:10	A1	
Detail sheet J: WC's	001/259	1:5,1:10	A1	
Detail sheet K: interface 1	001/260	1:5,1:10	A1	
Detail sheet K: interface 2	001/261	1:5,1:10	A1	
Schedule A: Doors	001/300	Nts	A3	
Schedule B: Windows	001/301	Nts	A3	
Schedule C: Ironmongery	001/302	Nts	A3	
Schedule D: Finishes	001/303	Nts	A3	
Schedule E: Sanitary	001/304	Nts	A3	
Schedule F: Manholes	001/305	Nts	A3	

DISTRIBUTION		NUMBER OF COPIES
	Client	
	Main. Contra.	
	Sub-Contractor	
	Sub-Contractor	
	Q.S	

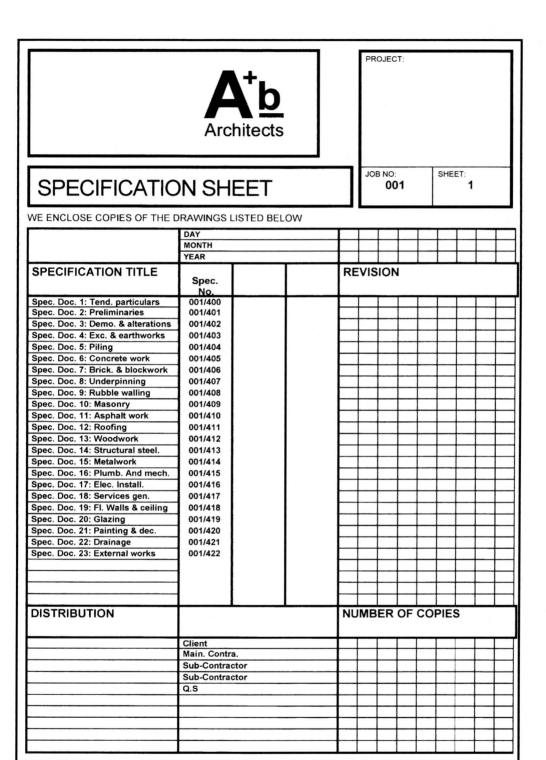

		DAY				REVISION									
		MONTH													
		YEAR													
SPECIFICATION TITLE		**Spec. No.**				**REVISION**									
Spec. Doc. 1: Tend. particulars		001/400													
Spec. Doc. 2: Preliminaries		001/401													
Spec. Doc. 3: Demo. & alterations		001/402													
Spec. Doc. 4: Exc. & earthworks		001/403													
Spec. Doc. 5: Piling		001/404													
Spec. Doc. 6: Concrete work		001/405													
Spec. Doc. 7: Brick. & blockwork		001/406													
Spec. Doc. 8: Underpinning		001/407													
Spec. Doc. 9: Rubble walling		001/408													
Spec. Doc. 10: Masonry		001/409													
Spec. Doc. 11: Asphalt work		001/410													
Spec. Doc. 12: Roofing		001/411													
Spec. Doc. 13: Woodwork		001/412													
Spec. Doc. 14: Structural steel.		001/413													
Spec. Doc. 15: Metalwork		001/414													
Spec. Doc. 16: Plumb. And mech.		001/415													
Spec. Doc. 17: Elec. Install.		001/416													
Spec. Doc. 18: Services gen.		001/417													
Spec. Doc. 19: Fl. Walls & ceiling		001/418													
Spec. Doc. 20: Glazing		001/419													
Spec. Doc. 21: Painting & dec.		001/420													
Spec. Doc. 22: Drainage		001/421													
Spec. Doc. 23: External works		001/422													

Specimen Value Assessment Sheet

Item	Criterion	Client weighting %	Marks awarded (out of 100)	Weighted marks
1. Technical	Technical proficiency	_____	_____	_____
	Innovation	_____	_____	_____
	Design skills	_____	_____	_____
	Relevant experience	_____	_____	_____
2. Management	Quality management systems in place	_____	_____	_____
	Ability to work successfully with clients to realise their objectives for the projects	_____	_____	_____
	Ability to work to programme	_____	_____	_____
	Ability to work to budget	_____	_____	_____
	Ability to work with other consultants and co-ordinate their work in design	_____	_____	_____
3. Method	Proposals for undertaking the work	_____	_____	_____
4. Staffing	Skills of the staff who will be working on the project, if known	_____	_____	_____
5. Location		_____	_____	_____
6. Facilities	Availability of relevant facilities such as computer aided design	_____	_____	_____
Total		_____	_____	_____

References

Allinson, K. (1993) *The Wild Card of Design* (Oxford: Butterworth-Heinemann).

Architect's Journal (AJ) (1995) [Centenary Issue].

Architects Journal (1998), 9 July, 45.

Ashworth, A. and Skitmore, R. M. (1982) Accuracy in estimating. CIOB Occasional Paper, No. 27.

Banwell, Sir H., Ministry of Public Building and Works, Committee on the Placing of Contracts for Building and Civil Engineering Work (1964) *The Placing and Management of Contracts for Building and Civil Engineering Work*. Report of the Committee (London: HMSO).

Beer, M. (1919) *History of British Socialism*, vol. 1 (London), p. 320.

Bellman, R. E. and Zadeh, L. A. (1970) Decision-making in a fuzzy management scene, 17(4), 141–64.

Bennett, J. and Jayes, S. (1995) *Trusting the Team: the Best Practice Guide to Partnering in Construction* (Reading: Reading Construction Forum, University of Reading).

Blackwood, D. J., Sarker, S. and Price, A. D. F. (1992) Planning and estimating design work – a review of British practice. In M. P. Nicholson (ed.), *Architectural Management* (London: E&FN Spon).

Booth, R. (2001) Indicative fee scales. *Architect's Journal (AJ)*, 8 March.

British Property Federation (BPF) (1983) *System for Building Design and Construction: Manual of the BPF System* (BPF).

Brook, M. (1998) *Estimating and Tendering for Construction Work* (Oxford: Butterworth-Heinemann).

Building Cost Information Service (BCIS), quarterly publications (London: RICS).

Building Cost Information Service (BCIS) (2001) *Review of Consultants' Fees on Construction Projects* (London: RICS).

Building Design (1995) Traditional procurement still the most popular. *Building Design*, 15 September, 5.

Campbell, R. (1747) *The London Tradesmen* (London).

Centre for Construction Market Information (1987) *Design and Building* (London: CCMI).

Chambers, W. and Chambers, R. (1983) *Chambers New Edition Dictionary* (Edinburgh: Chambers).

Chappell, D. and Willis, A. (2000) *The Architect in Practice* (Oxford: Blackwell).

CIC and RIBA (1999) *Engaging an Architect: Guidance for Clients to Quality Based Selection* (London: CIC and RIBA).

CIOB (1997) *Code of Estimating Practice* (Harlow: Addison-Wesley Longman).

Clamp, H. (1993) *The Shorter Forms of Building Contract*, 3rd edn (Oxford: Blackwell), p. 82.

Coles, E. J. (1992) Planning building design work. In M. P. Nicholson (ed.), *Architectural Management* (London: E&FN Spon).

Cooper, R. and Press, M. (1998) *The Design Agenda: A Guide to Successful Design Management* (Chichester: Wiley).

Daschbach, J. M. and Agpar, H. (1988) Design analysis through techniques of parametric cost estimation. *Engineering Costs and Production Economics*, no. 14, 87–93.

Deming, W. E. (1986) *Out of the Crisis* (Cambridge, MA: MIT Press).

Denning, J. (1992) Design and build goes public. *Civil Engineering, ASCE*, 62(7).

Dormer, P. (1991) *The Meaning of Modern Design* (New York: Thames & Hudson).

Egan, J. (1998) *Rethinking Construction* (London: HMSO).

Ellegant, H. (1992) Modern value engineering for design and construction. In M. P. Nicholson (ed.), *Architectural Management* (London: E&FN Spon), pp. 247–55.

Emmerson, Sir H. (1962) *Survey of Problems before the Construction Industries* (London: HMSO).

Emmitt, S. and Neary, S. (1995) The change agent – a role for CPD in a competitive environment. In M. P. Nicholson (ed.), *Architectural Management Practice and Research*, Amsterdam (Nottingham: SAAM).

Erwin, G. J., Bowen, P. A. and Strez, H. A. (1991) The treatment of uncertainty in the building procurement process using expert system-based techniques. In *Proceedings of Construction Project Modelling*, Dubrovnik, CIB (Nottingham: SAAM).

Evemy, M. (1990) Designs on construction. *New Builder*, April.

Lord Foster of Thameside (1999) *Daily Telegraph*, 16 January.

Fox, J. (1986) Knowledge, decision-making and uncertainty. In Gale (ed.), *Artificial Intelligence and Statistics*, pp. 57–76.

Franks, J. (1984) *Building Procurement Systems – A Guide to Building Project Management* (Ascot: CIOB).

Gray, C. (1994) Iterative design – essential or poor management? In M. P. Nicholson (ed.), *Architectural Management Practice and Research* (Nottingham: SAAM).

Gray, C., Hughes, W. and Bennett, J. (1994) *The Successful Management of Design* (Reading: University of Reading).

Green, S. D. (1994) Beyond value engineering: SMART value management for building projects. *International Journal of Project Management*, 12(1), 49–56.

Gruneberg, S. L. (ed.) (1995) Responding to Latham: the views of the construction team. In *Proceedings of the Latham Report Conference* (London: South Bank University).

The Guardian (1962) Communion. The report of the building of a church. *The Guardian*, 6 December.

Hamilton, A. (ed.) (1995) *The Brooks Method of Architect Selection* (London: RIBA).

Heap, J. (1989) *The Management of Innovation and Design* (London: Cassell).

Higgins, G. and Jessop, N. (1965) *Communications in the Building Industry* (London: Tavistock Institute).

Hillman, J. (1992) *Medics and the Millennium, Government Patronage and Architecture* (London: HMSO for the Royal Fine Art Commission).

HM Treasury (1997) *Procurement Guidance. No. 2: Value for Money in Construction Procurement* (London: Treasury's Public Enquiry Unit).

Houldsworth, H. K. (1983) Building industry employers' and trades' associations 1833–1884. Unpublished MPhil thesis, University of Nottingham.

Hyams, D. (2001) *Construction Companion 'Briefing'* (London: RIBA).

Jepson, W. B. and Nicholson, M. P. (1972) *Marketing and Building Management* (Lancaster: MTP).

Jones, E. (2000) *The Observer*, 12 March.

Jones, J. C. (1970) *Design Methods: Seeds of Human Futures* (New York: Wiley).

Kwakye A. A. (1991a) Fast tracking construction procurement. *Chartered Builder*, October.

Kwakye, A. A. (1991b) Construction by Fast Tracking. Occasional Paper, No. 46 (Ascot: CIOB).

Latham, M. (1994) *Constructing the Team* (London: HMSO).

Lawson, B. R. (1994) *Design in Mind* (Oxford: Butterworth Architecture).

Lawson, B. R. (1997) *How Designers Think* (Oxford: Architectural Press).

LeGood, J. R. (2000) Letter to the Editor. *Architect's Journal*, 23 March.

Mandani, E. H. and Efstathiou, H. J. (1985) Higher order logics for handling uncertainty in expert systems. *International Journal of Man–Machine Studies*, 93, 283–93.

McArtney, T. (2000) Letter to the Editor. *Architect's Journal*, 16 March.

McLellan, M. (1994) Fee bidding surge puts squeeze on standards. *New Builder*, 25 March.

Ministry of Works (1944) *Pricing of Building Contracts* (London: HMSO), pp. 19–21.

Mirza & Nacey Research (2000) *Architects' Fees – A Survey of the Fees Charged by Private Architectural Practices* (Arundel: Mirza & Nacey Research <www.architectsfees.co.uk>).

Naamani, Z. (1990) Management techniques and computer applications in architecture. Unpublished PhD thesis, University of Nottingham.

Ndekugri, I. and Turner, A. (1994) Building procurement by design and build approach. *ASCE Journal of Construction Engineering and Management*, 120(2), 120–2.

NEDC (1983) *Faster Building for Industry* (London: HMSO for Building EDC).

Norris, C. (1992) *Project Risk, Analysis and Management* (Aylesbury: Association of Project Managers).

Ogunlana, S. O. (1989) Accuracy in design cost estimating. Unpublished PhD thesis, Loughborough University of Technology.

Organisation for Economic Co-operation & Development (OECD) (1985) Organisation for Economic Co-operation & Development Report.

Pawley, M. (1998) Yes, we have no competition. *Architect's Journal (AJ)*, 16 April.

Pepperell, N. T. and Cecil, R. (c.1990) *Risk Management for Architects* (London: RIBA Indemnity Research).

Petroski, H. (1996) *Invention by Design – How Engineers Get from Thought to Thing* (Cambridge, MA: Harvard University Press).

Phillips (1950) *Phillips Report* (London: HMSO).

Pilkington (1956) *Pilkington Report* (London: HMSO).

Popovic, O. and Nicholson, M. P. (1993) In M. P. Nicholson (ed.), *Architectural Management Practice and Research*, Rotterdam, CIB (Nottingham: SAAM).

Potter D. and Scions D. (1982) *Computer-aided Estimating*. Paper No. 7. CIOB Technical Information Papers (Ascot: CIOB).

RIBA (1872) *Conditions of Engagement and Scale of Professional Charges* (London: RIBA).

RIBA (1962) *The Architect and His Office* (London: RIBA).

RIBA (1970) *Architects' Handbook' – Plan of Work* (London: RIBA).

RIBA (1973) *Plan of Work* (London: RIBA).

RIBA (1982) *The Architect's Appointment* (London: RIBA).

RIBA (1986) *Tendering for Architects' Services* (London: RIBA).

RIBA (1990) *Architects' Appointment* (London: RIBA).

RIBA (1992) *Standard Form of Agreement for the Appointment of an Architect*. SFA/92 (London: RIBA).

RIBA (1994) *Guidance for Clients on Fees: Engaging an Architect* (London: RIBA).

RIBA (1995a) *Conditions of Engagement for the Appointment of an Architect*. CE/95 (London: RIBA).

RIBA (1995b) *Strategic Study, Phases 3 & 4* (London: RIBA); first published *RIBA Journal* (1994), November.

RIBA (1999a) *A Client's Guide to Engaging an Architect – Including Guidance on Fees* (London: RIBA).

RIBA (1999b) *Conditions of Engagement for the Appointment of an Architect*. CE/99 (London: RIBA).

RIBA (1999c) *Engaging an Architect: Guidance for Clients to Quality-based Selection* (London: RIBA).

RIBA (1999d) *Standard Form of Agreement for the Appointment of an Architect*. SFA/99 (London: RIBA).

RIBA (2000) *Architect's Plan of Work* (London: RIBA).

RIBA (2001) *Architects' Employment and Earnings 2001* (London: RIBA).

Richardson, V. (2001) Fees survey. *RIBA Journal*, October.

Saint, A. (1983) *The Image of the Architect* (New Haven and London: Yale University Press).

Sawczuk, B. (1996) *Risk Avoidance for the Building Team* (London: E&FN Spon).

Saxon, R. (2000) *Architect's Journal*, 3 February.

Schneider, E., and Davies, H. (1995) *Strategic Study, Phases 3 & 4, Breaking Out of the Mould* (London: RIBA); first published *Architect's Journal* (1995), April.

Sher, W. (1996) *Computer-aided Estimating* (Harlow: Addison-Wesley Longman).

Schroge, M. (2000) *Serious Play: How the World's Best Companies Simulate to Innovate* (Boston: Harvard College Press).

Simon, Sir E. (1944) *The Placing and Management of Building Works* (London: Simon HMSO).

SMM (Standard Method of Measurement of Building Works) (London: RICS).

Songer, A. D. and Ibbs, C. W. (1995) Managing a request for proposal developments in public sector design and build. In Moreledge, R. (ed.), *Journal of Construction Procurement*.

Spain, B. (ed.) (2000) *Spon's First Stage Estimating Handbook* (London: E&FN Spon).

Spekkink, D. (1993) *The Client's Brief: More than a Questionnaire*. Proceedings of CIB W96 Architectural Management, Eindhoven, April (Nottingham: SAAM).

Spon (2000) *Spon's Architects' & Builders' Price Book* (London: E&FN Spon).

Summitters, C. E. (1992) C. E. Summitters offers views on problems troubling the profession. *Civil Engineering, ASCE*, 8, 62.

Symes M, Eley, J. and Seidel A. D. (1995) *Architects and their Practices – A Changing Profession* (Oxford: Butterworth Architecture).

Thomke, S. and Tekahiro, F. (1998) 'The effect of frontloading problem solving on product development performance'. Working Paper, Harvard Business School, Boston, MA, December.

Thompson, A. (1997) *Architectural Design Procedures* (London: Edward Arnold).

Toole, M. (1990) Design work by sub-contractors. *Construction Law*, 1(April).

Topalian, A. (1989) Organisational features that nurture design success in enterprises. In Proceedings of the 2nd International Conference on Engineering Management, Toronto.

Topalian, A. (1994) Best practice benchmarking of design management practices and performance. In *The Alto Design Management Workbook* (London: author at Alto Design Management).

Walker, C. (2001) Labour's jail threat to architects. *Architect's Journal (AJ)*, 21 June.

Whitfield, P. R. (1975) *Creativity in Industry* (Harmondsworth: Penguin).

Williams, A. (2001) Drive for improvement. *Architect's Journal (AJ)*, 26 July.

Wimpey Construction UK (1990) Consultancy Agreement. Clause 4.3.

Wright, H. (2000) Letter to the Editor. *Architect's Journal*, 23 March.

Index